THIRD EDITION

STYLE

Ten Lessons in Clarity & Grace

JOSEPH M. WILLIAMS
University of Chicago

SCOTT, FORESMAN AND COMPANY

Glenview, Illinois   Boston   London

Literary acknowledgments appear on page 237, which constitutes a legal extension of the copyright page.

Copyright © 1989, 1985, 1981 Scott, Foresman and Company.
All Rights Reserved.
Printed in the United States of America.

Library of Congress Cataloging in Publication Data
Williams, Joseph M.
   Style : ten lessons in clarity and grace / Joseph M. Williams. 3rd ed.
    p.   cm.
   Includes index.
   ISBN 0-673-38186-2
   1. English language—Rhetoric. 2. English language—Style.
3. English language—Business English. 4. English language—
Technical English. I. Title.
PE1421.W545 1989   88-18548
808'.042—dc19   CIP

456-KPF-92919089

... English style, familiar but not coarse,
elegant but not ostentatious ...

Samuel Johnson

To my mother and father

PREFACE

To Those Who Write on the Job

Fortunately, most of you require no convincing about the importance of a clear and readable style, especially if you have to waste a large part of your day struggling through the prose of those who have never learned to write well. Unfortunately, the advice that most of us recall about writing well probably doesn't help us correct even our own bad writing. If what we remember is typical of most such advice, it probably consists of banalities such as "Be clear, be concise," or of useless minutiae such as "Don't begin sentences with *and* or end them with prepositions."

The kind of confused writing that most of us have to live with fails for reasons that don't yield to well-meant but empty generalities or to any list of particular dos and don'ts. To understand why anyone—including ourselves—writes badly, we have to be able to look at a sentence and understand how it works, how the ideas have been distributed through its different parts, and then decide how to write it better.

To address that problem, we have to be specific and concrete, and that means we have to use some of those terms we may or may not remember from junior high school—*verb, object, noun, active, passive,* and so on. Every subject has a vocabulary which anyone learning that subject has to master. It's the same with style: If you want to understand and improve your own, you have to control a few terms. There aren't a lot of them here, they're not difficult, and every one of them is defined in the Glossary. Under no circumstances waste your time trying to memorize them. Simply learning how to define nouns and verbs won't help you write any better. But if you can develop a sense of how nouns and verbs differ, you'll understand what distinguishes good and bad writing, and *that* will help you write better.

Something I have found repeatedly among those who have a problem with the way people in their organization write is the lack of a common language about writing and its problems. If you are responsible for the writing of others and you find it unacceptable, you have to communicate to those writers more than your displeasure. You have to tell them what to do to write better. Yet time and again administrators simply ignore the problem because they don't feel confident discussing style: Neither the administrator nor the subordinate has a vocabulary to express what either sees as the source of the difficulty. Or if an administrator does try to explain what's wrong, his or her language is vague, impressionistic, and different from the language of others in the organization who must also tell their subordinates how to improve their writing.

This book provides the consistent and explicit vocabulary that will let you address a writing problem consistently and explicitly.

To Students

Nothing is more tedious than learning a skill that seems to have no immediate application and no obvious value, even in the distant future. You've already learned how to write well enough to get as far as you've come. And when you read all those textbooks, journal articles, and scholarly monographs written in language so turgid and incomprehensible that it sets one's head to throbbing, the penalty for bad writing must seem to be not especially severe. If someone can write badly and still get published, why should any of us spend the time and effort learning how to write well?

The answer is one that you will have to take partly on faith: First, and most obviously, the very scarcity of clear and precise writing makes it that much more valuable. Even though an unclear and imprecise style obviously does not bar a good many writers from getting into print, a person who can write clearly and gracefully goes out into the world with an uncommon skill. One important reason business people and professionals do not achieve what their potential might otherwise allow is their inability to communicate, to get their good ideas down on paper in a way that lets others understand those ideas quickly and easily. In every survey that asks business people what subjects they wish they had studied more carefully, their first or second answer is always communication.

True, you might compensate for a turgid style with great ideas, with an original and creative mind. But the more common truth is that most of us have minds and ideas that are closer to merely good than to outstandingly brilliant. And ideas that are only good need all the help they can get. So if we weren't born brilliant, we can at least learn to be clear; it is, in fact, an ability that is just as rare as inherited genius, and most of the time considerably more useful.

I know how unpersuasive this kind of "let-me-tell-you-what's-good-for-you" argument is before you've tested it against hard experience. But in fact, you may already have conducted the test: How often have you wanted to toss aside a textbook or journal article whose every leaden sentence was an agony to read? How many sentences have you reread and reread again, struggling to extract whatever meaning may or may not have sunk under the weight of all that verbiage? How often have you read a dozen pages only to realize that you can't recall a single idea?

You have to read that kind of writing now, perhaps because it's been assigned, perhaps because you need it for a term paper. But suppose for a moment that you were the boss of someone who wrote badly, and that you've just received a memo or report written in that tangled, abstract style. What do you think would be your first impulse?

Finally, the tone of this book is strongly prescriptive. Its lessons will tell you in a straightforward way how to write clearly. I think the advice is sound. I've tested it with a good many adult writers in government, the professions, and business. So far, no one has objected that the problems we will be addressing are irrelevant to the concerns that real writers have in the real world. Quite the contrary: They go to the flabby heart of a terminally opaque style.

But however prescriptive I seem about what counts as clear writing, don't you be reluctant to experiment, to play with different prose styles. Try writing in the ponderous bureaucratic style that this book condemns, simply to get the feel of writing it. Try creating a passage in a style elegant beyond your needs, just to see whether you can pull it off. Try writing the longest sentence you can, just to feel when you've stretched it to its breaking point. Try writing a passage of one curt sentence after another to achieve a sense of breathless haste, or of utter certitude.

Language, style, should not be something that boxes you in, but a means to free your intellect and imagination from the obscurity that confused prose puts between you and your ideas.

To Teachers

This book addresses only one aspect of composition: style. It does not take up matters of intention, invention, or organization. Their omission is not an oversight. I intend this to be a short book that focuses on the single most serious problem that *mature* writers face: a wordy, tangled, too-complex prose style. For larger matters of form, you will need another book.

I have tried to approach style as process, as an achievement. The first step, of course, is to get something down on paper. But that's the easy part. The serious part of writing is rewriting. Samuel Johnson said it about as well as anyone: "What is written without effort is in general read without pleasure." The effort is more in the editing than in the writing.

I know that many undergraduates have a problem precisely opposite to that which most of this book addresses—a style characterized by one fifteen-word sentence after another. But that's not a problem that endures very long. I have worked with many adult writers in government, in the professions, in business; I have met not one whose major writing problem was a style that was immature. I am encouraged in this observation by every other adult writing program I have ever seen: Not one of them takes up the matter of writing longer rather than shorter sentences.

Now, you might object that there is still no point in addressing a problem that does not yet afflict your students. Two points: First, dealing with this matter now will prepare them to deal with it later. To assume that we should not address a problem before it arises is a little bit like teaching birth control after the rabbit dies.

And second, simply by writing out the new sentences that result from editing those in the exercises, students will come to feel what it is like to write down a sentence longer than ten or fifteen words. Copy and imitation, time-honored ways of teaching writing, will help the less advanced students feel the rhythm and movement that a long but clear sentence demands. After all, if we cannot lead our students through what they are supposed to be learning to do, we ought not be surprised when they do not learn to do it.

The exercises in imitation are directed specifically toward developing a mature style. Assure your students that they don't have to imitate the model sentences word for word; they have only to imitate the stylistic point being discussed. If they have problems thinking up things to write about, suggest some topics parallel to the subject matter of the model sentences. In fact, you might do the exercises yourself to get a sense of what can and can't be done with them.

All this is intended to anticipate an objection that some readers may raise: The material is appropriate for upper-class students and adults but too difficult for beginning students. I understand why some teachers of freshmen might feel that way. I realize how severely underprepared many first-year students are in matters of both style and grammar. I use a few grammatical terms here. But I confess I am a bit puzzled that any teacher would object to a discussion that introduces terms that a student does not know but should. I have always assumed that we are in the business of teaching students what they do not know, and that if they do not know what *subject, verb, predicate, object,* and so on mean, then we tell them. I don't see how we can avoid using some terminology, even new terminology, any more than a physicist can avoid using new terms such as *lepton, quark,* or *charmed particle* in a textbook on the structure of matter.

Lesson Ten on style and usage may disconcert more than a few. (Indeed, it already has.) It asserts that some widely circulated "rules" of usage may in fact not be as widely observed by genuinely careful writers as some might think, or wish. Parts of that lesson may read as if I based my observations on some quirky notions of personal usage, privately arrived at. In fact, I have based them on a good deal of reading, done specifically to find whether those "rules" have any force among otherwise careful writers. I can only assert that in writing which has not been thoroughly edited to make it conform to the "rules" I address, there appear a good many singular *datas,* a good many *whiches* for *thats,* a good many prepositions at the ends of sentences, split infinitives, sentences beginning with *and.* Indeed, all these so-called violations of good usage appear in books that have been scrupulously edited.

In the real world of real writers, success depends little on avoiding *contact* as verb or *finalize* meaning more than finish. It depends on the ability to make a point precisely, directly, and persuasively.

"Precision" and "Upholding Standards" have too often meant finding trivial points of usage violated in prose that deserves criticism on far more substantial grounds. Coming down hard on a *which* that we think should be a *that* has for too long been a way of saying, "I don't like what I'm reading very much, but I don't know how else to express my dislike." It is the equivalent of that all-purpose "Awk" that so many among us scribble in the margin when they can't explain what *makes* a sentence awkward.

I hope that what follows will provide a vocabulary that makes the word *precision* more than an expression of imprecise values, and *imprecise* more often an expression of precise displeasure.

To All

Devoured in one piece, this book will surely seem indigestible. It does not have the leisurely pace of an occasional essay that can be read in one or two sittings. Take the lessons in small chunks. Do a section at a time, up to the exercises. Do the exercises; find someone else's writing to edit; edit some writing of your own. Then look hard at what you've written today—first only for the point of the lesson, or section. Then go through it again, looking for another point, and if you have the time, again for other points. If you try to edit everything at once, a sentence will dissolve into a confusion of words.

So many have provided useful criticism and welcome support that I cannot possibly thank them all. But I must begin with my English 194 students, who put up with so many badly typed and faintly dittoed pages and with a teacher who was at times as puzzled over matters of style as they. Their interest in clear and concise writing compensated for a lot of tedious hours spent editing their papers. They were a pleasure to teach, and their subsequent comments about the importance of what they have learned have been gratifying. I thank them all.

I have considerable intellectual debts to those who have broken ground in psycholinguistics, text linguistics, discourse analysis, functional sentence perspective, and so on. Those of you who keep up with such matters will recognize the influence of Charles Fillmore, Jan Firbas, Nils Enkvist, Michael Halliday, Noam Chomsky, Thomas Bever, Vic Yngve, and others. I know I have been influenced more than a little by Robert Graves and Alan Hodge, H. W. Fowler, H. L. Mencken, and surely by E. B. White. I would like to think that I have made explicit what Mr. White advises writers to do and what he himself has done for so long. Maine air must be, I think, a powerful astringent to style.

I am very grateful to colleagues who have taken time from their own busy lives to read the work of another. At such times, the word *community* in Community of Scholars takes on a special meaning. Whatever quality this book may have is due in large part to their care, time, and energy. I must thank in particular Randy Berlin, Ken Bruffee, Douglas Butturff, Donald Byker, Bruce Campbell, Elaine Chaika, Avon Crismore, Don Freeman, Constance Gefvert, Maxine Hairston, George Hoffman, Ted Lowe, Susan Miller, Neil Nakadate, Mike Pownall, Peter Priest, Margaret Shaklee, Nancy Sommers, Mary Taylor, and Stephen Witte.

I would also like to acknowledge the assistance of Frederick C. Mish, editorial director, G. & C. Merriam Company, in locating the best examples of three citations in Lesson Ten.

The editors at Scott, Foresman saved me from more than a few stylistic gaffes, especially Dave Ebbitt, whose editing pen has a very sharp point.

I would like to thank most profoundly the editor who first urged me to write this book, Harriett Prentiss. I am most grateful to her.

And finally, to my family—my thanks for your love and support and understanding, especially when Daddy's "just one minute" stretched to an hour or two.

Joseph M. Williams

PREFACE TO THE THIRD EDITION

While I would like to think that I may finally be getting this thing close to right, I know too that I may seem only to be tinkering at it. A few have suggested that *Style₃* end on something more inspiring than commas and semicolons, so I've moved to the end the Lesson on Usage. The Lesson on Special Problems should have been from the first folded into Lessons One and Two, so I did that, too. There is some new material. And with the help of three very careful editors, I've cleaned up some of the fuzzier passages. By his mercilessly scrupulous reading, Dave Ebbitt once again proved himself to be someone I would cheerfully impale on his editing pencil. That I have not accepted all of his suggestions speaks to which of us is more stiff-necked. The Rajalas, Constance and Hope, were gentler but no less strict in their attention to detail. I am grateful to all three for their unqualified professionalism. My thanks to Theresa Dougal whose discerning eye caught a good many errors that I missed. For some detailed observations about *Style₂* I am also grateful to Carolyn Collette, Mary Coney, David Cunningham, Jeanne Fahnestock, Mary Gilliam, Ian Leask, Harriet Ritvo, Sally Spurgin, James Stratman, and Margaret Urie, and to several others whose letters have disappeared into the Black Hole of my desktop, but who will see herein the benefit of their generous interest. I apologize to you all for not acknowledging you by name; I am twice over in your debt.

I can acknowledge by name, though, six who by their inimitable styles have contributed mightily to the quality of my life: In alphabetical order, Chris, Dave, Joe, Megan, and Oliver. And at beginning and end, Joan.

J.M.W.

CONTENTS

Toward Clarity

Everything that can be thought at all can be thought clearly. Everything that can be said can be said clearly.

LUDWIG WITTGENSTEIN

Have something to say, and say it as clearly as you can. That is the only secret of style.

MATTHEW ARNOLD

The great enemy of clear language is insincerity. . . .

GEORGE ORWELL

In matters of grave importance, style, not sincerity, is the vital thing.

OSCAR WILDE

With precious few exceptions, all the books on style in English are by writers quite unable to write.

H. L. MENCKEN

This is a short book based on a simple thesis: it's good to write clearly, and anyone can.

No one would argue with the first part of that claim, least of all those who regularly have to translate prose like this:

> There is now no effective mechanism for introducing into the initiation and development stages of reporting requirements information on existing reporting and guidance on how to minimize burden associations with new requirements.

But that second part might seem a bit too optimistic for those who have labored to write clearly and still bring forth a tangle of prose that hides their ideas not only from their readers, but sometimes even from themselves.

Now, we can write prose that fails for reasons more important than an obscure style. If we're as confused about a point when we finish a job of writing as when we began, our writing will be confused too. If we ignore what our readers have to know if they're to understand our ideas, then what we write will surely bewilder them. And if we can't find a way to organize our ideas clearly, then what we write will almost certainly lack that sense of direction and purpose that all coherent prose demands.

But important as those problems are, this book addresses a different matter: Once we've learned how to write sentences that are grammatically correct and acceptably punctuated, once we've learned how to focus our ideas, how to gather and organize the information we need to move a clearly defined audience to a specific end, we still have to get those ideas down on paper in a form that is not just correct, but clear and concise enough to be effective.

That is the aim of this book: to explain how you can overcome a problem that has afflicted generations of mature writers—the problem of an unnecessarily complex prose style. When we find this kind of writing in government regulations and directives, we call it *bureaucratese;* when we find it in contracts and judicial pronouncements, we call it *legalese;* when we find it in scholarly articles and books that inflate simple ideas into gassy abstractions, we call it *academese.* Partly because we find it almost everywhere, some believe that it must be the style of institutional success. It is more often the style of academic pretension or bureaucratic intimidation. Wherever we find it, it is a style that, once we see through it, must finally infuriate us.

Anyone familiar with the history of English prose has to wonder whether we can do anything that will substantially improve it. In the early sixteenth century, when English first became respectable enough to replace French and Latin as England's institutional language, our first impulse toward elegance produced a prose style thick with Latinate abstraction, a weakness to which many English writers have surrendered ever since.

By the middle of the seventeenth century, an inflated style had infected the sciences. Shortly after the Royal Society was established in 1660, one of its historians complained.

> ... of all the studies of men, nothing may sooner be obtained than this vicious abundance of phrase, this trick of metaphors, this volubility of tongue which makes so great a noise in the world. . . .
> —Thomas Sprat, *History of the Royal Society,* 1667

When the New World was settled, we had a chance to create a lean and sinewy prose style suitable for a people civilizing a continent. But American writers no more escaped chronic bloat and abstraction than did the English. James Fenimore Cooper asserted, none too simply himself, that "the common faults of American language are an ambition of effect, a want of simplicity, and a turgid abuse of terms." Henry David Thoreau agreed: "All men are really attracted by the beauty of plain speech [but they] write in a florid style in imitation of this."

We read the same sentiments today. On the language of the social sciences:

> ... a turgid and polysyllabic prose does seem to prevail in the social sciences. . . . Such a lack of ready intelligibility, I believe, usually has little or nothing to do with the complexity of thought. It has to do almost entirely with certain confusions of the academic writer about his own status.
> —C. Wright Mills, *The Sociological Imagination*

On the language of medicine:

> It now appears that obligatory obfuscation is a firm tradition within the medical profession. . . . [Medical writing] is a highly skilled, calculated attempt to confuse the reader. . . . A doctor feels he might get passed over for an assistant professorship because he wrote his papers too clearly—because he made his ideas seem too simple.
> —Michael Crichton, *New England Journal of Medicine*

And on the language of law:

> ... in law journals, in speeches, in classrooms and in courtrooms,
> lawyers and judges are beginning to worry about how often they
> have been misunderstood, and they are discovering that sometimes
> they cannot even understand each other.
> —Tom Goldstein, *New York Times*

(The abuse heaped on the prose of government bureaucrats is too familiar to need special testimony here.)

Most adults, I suspect, write in these ways for some combination of just two or three reasons. Michael Crichton cited the first: We use complicated language not only to dress up simple ideas but to hide the absence of any ideas. Impenetrable prose will impress those who confuse difficulty with substance—and there are many who do. Why else so much turgid writing?

In the same way, we use difficult and therefore intimidating language to protect what we have from those who want a share of it: the power, prestige, and privilege that go with being part of the ruling class. We can conceal knowledge by locking it up, but we can also hide ideas behind language so impenetrable that only those trained to translate it can find them.

Another reason some of us write badly is that we are seized by the memory of an English teacher for whom the only good writing was writing free from errors which only that teacher could understand: fused genitives, dangling participles, split infinitives, and other exotic *disjecta membra*. For many such writers, a blank page is now a minefield they traverse gingerly, concerned less with clarity and precision than with sheer survival.

But the most common reason for bad writing is, I think, the simplest: Most writers have just never learned how to write clearly and directly in the first place. No one has ever told them how to edit syntactic confusion into clear prose. Or even that they should try. I say this because I have never met anyone who was anything but delighted to learn the few simple principles needed to edit an unreadable tangle into clear, straightforward prose.

Now, in fact, when we address this matter of clear prose, we indirectly address some of those more general problems that I referred to before—problems of organization, intention, and audience. The very act of writing and rewriting helps us to clarify our ideas, to understand better what we want to say, to find the best way to organize our material, to speak to the real interests and needs of our readers. If we can't see through our own confused style to the substance of our ideas, we won't be able to understand ourselves well enough to use the act of writing to sharpen our ideas, our organization, and our intentions. When we write page after page of impenetrable prose, we finally lose track of our train of thought: The mere effort to find our way through every sentence finally distracts us from the substance of our ideas.

Writing can be a fruitfully circular process: We have to understand what we want to say in order to write it clearly and concisely. But if we can't write what we mean clearly and concisely enough or, when necessary, clearly though complexly enough, we won't be able to understand exactly what we should be saying. If we can write and then quickly rewrite syntactic confusion into clear prose, we'll understand our ideas better. And when we understand our ideas better, we'll write more clearly, and if we write more clearly, we'll understand even better . . . and so it goes, until we run out of energy, interest, or time.

For some of us, that moment may come months or years after we begin. But for most of us, it's closer to tomorrow morning. Few of us enjoy the luxury of ruminating for weeks and months over our prose, polishing every phrase and clause to a lapidary finish. Most of us have to be satisfied with an imperfect but still useful product.

That limitation only makes a clear, direct style more important: If we don't have the time to ponder over every sentence as we write, we have to be able to get our ideas down quickly and surely the first time, and then to edit our first draft into something clear, simple, and direct.

As important as directness and clarity may be, there are times when we want to go beyond it, to a style that is a bit more self-conscious, to a style that may even be just a bit elegant.

> Now the trumpet summons us again—not as a call to bear arms,
> though arms we need; not as a call to battle, though embattled we
> are; but a call to bear the burden of a long twilight struggle, year in
> and year out, "rejoicing in hope, patient in tribulation," a struggle
> against the common enemies of man: tyranny, poverty, disease and
> war itself.
> —John F. Kennedy, Inaugural Address, January 20, 1961

Not all of us are called upon to write a Presidential Inaugural Address, but sometimes our intentions, our sense of who we are, require that we invest even our most modest prose with more than simple clarity. The last few lessons in this book speak to that matter.

About fifty years ago, H. L. Mencken wrote,

> With precious few exceptions, all the books on style in English are by writers quite unable to write. The subject, indeed, seems to exercise a special and dreadful fascination over school ma'ams, bucolic college professors, and other such pseudoliterates . . . Their central aim, of course, is to reduce the whole thing to a series of simple rules—the overmastering passion of their melancholy order, at all times and everywhere.

This melancholy judgment has hovered over every sentence I've written here. And Mencken was right: No one can teach a clear style by rule, simple or not, especially to those who have nothing to say and no reason to say it, to those who cannot think or feel or see.

But I know that many do think carefully and feel deeply and see clearly but still cannot write well. I also know that learning to write well can help us think and feel and see, and that in fact there are some simple and straightforward principles that help.

Here they are.

The Grammar of Clarity

Suit the action to the word, the word to the action.
WILLIAM SHAKESPEARE, *Hamlet*, 3.2

Action is eloquence.
WILLIAM SHAKESPEARE, *Coriolanus*, 3.2

Words and deeds are quite different modes of the divine energy. Words are also actions, and actions are a kind of words.
RALPH WALDO EMERSON

We have words enough to praise writing that we like, and more than enough to abuse writing we don't. What we like we call clear, direct, concise, flowing, readable; the other we call turgid, indirect, unclear, unreadable, confusing, abstract, awkward, disjointed, opaque, complex, impersonal, wordy, prolix, obscure, inflated, pompous, and so on. They are among the words we could use to describe these two sentences:

> Our lack of pertinent data prevented determination of committee action effectiveness in the targeting of funds to those areas in greatest assistance need.

> Because we lacked pertinent data, we could not determine whether the committee had targeted funds to areas that needed assistance the most.

But when I use a word like *turgid* for the first sentence or *clear* for the second, I describe only how those sentences make me feel. What I call *turgid* isn't on the page. *Turgid* names a thick feeling behind my eyes. The problem with accounting for style is that we need a way not only to describe how a passage makes us feel. We need a way to connect those feelings to what it is *on the page* that explains why we feel as we do.

Some ways to measure clarity, for example, have us count syllables and words (the fewer the better, according to most such schemes). But if we counted every syllable and word in every sentence we wrote, we'd spend more time counting than writing. And even if counting did tell us which of those two sentences was more or less easy to read, we wouldn't have to count if we could sense when a passage was clear and direct or tangled and obscure in the first place. Even more important, numbers don't tell us how to write a clear sentence—or, more importantly, how to revise a turgid one.

The difference between those two sentences doesn't depend on numbers of words or syllables. The sentences differ in the way the writer used subjects and verbs to tell a story. Subjects and verbs—those words and a few others are all the vocabulary we'll need to understand and explain why those two sentences make us feel as we do. Then we can explain how to revise the turgidity of that first sentence into the clarity of the second.

TELLING STORIES

In almost everything we write we tell a story. Prose that may seem wholly abstract usually has behind it a story in which real characters act:

Our estimate is of a 50% reduction in the introduction of our chemical products in the event that compliance with the Preliminary Manufacturing Notice is made a requirement under proposed Federal legislation.

If **Congress** requires that **we** comply with the Preliminary Manufacturing Notice, **we** estimate that **we** will introduce 50% fewer chemical products.

It may even be a story whose buried main characters are concepts:

The scientific status of evolutionary theory has widespread relationships with so many aspects of current thinking in other fields of scientific research that only the falsification of those other fields would result in its surrender to creationism.

Because **evolutionary theory** relates to so **many other fields of scientific research, it** will yield to **creationism** only when **those other fields** prove false.

THE FIRST PRINCIPLE OF CLEAR WRITING

When we link the simple point that sentences are stories about characters who act to the way we use the grammar of a sentence to describe those characters and their actions, we get a principle of style more powerful than any other. It is a principle that explains how turgid prose really differs from clear prose; but more important, it also tells us how to revise one into the other. Here's the principle. It has two parts: (all grammatical terms are defined in the glossary).

(1) In the subjects of your sentences, name your cast of characters.
(2) In the verbs of your sentences, name the crucial actions in which you involve those characters.

For example, look again at that first sentence on p. 8:

Our lack of pertinent data prevented determination of committee action effectiveness in the targeting of funds to those areas in greatest assistance need.

Who are the characters? Push the dramatic metaphor a step: if we were to cast this sentence as an opera, how many parts would we have to fill? There is a "we" (in the form of *our*); there is "the committee" (are its members the same as "we?"); and there are the "areas." But where in that first sentence do those characters appear? *Our* is not a subject, but a modifier of *lack: our lack. Committee* is not a subject, but another modifier, *committee action effectiveness.* And *areas* is not a subject either, but the object of a preposition: *to areas.* What is the subject of this sentence? An abstraction: *Our lack of pertinent data,* with its general verb *precluded.*

Now look at the second sentence:

> Because we lacked pertinent data, we could not determine whether the committee had targeted funds to areas that needed assistance the most.

We is the subject of both *lack* and *could not determine.*

> *Because we lacked . . . , we could not determine . . .*

The committee is the subject of the verb *had targeted:*

> *the committee had targeted.*

Finally, although *area* is still the object of a preposition: *to areas,* it is also the subject of *needed.*

> *areas that needed assistance the most.*

The first sentence consistently violates the first half of our principle: use subjects to name your cast of characters. The second sentence consistently observes it.

Now look at how the two sentences name the actions associated with the characters. In the first, the actions are not verbs, but rather abstract nouns: *lack, determination, action, targeting, assistance, need.* The second consistently names those actions in verbs: *we lacked, we could not determine, the committee targeted, areas needed.* The only action still a noun is *assistance.*

So the first sentence also violates the second half of our principle: Express actions as verbs. And again, the second observes it.

The real difference between those sentences lies not in their numbers, but in how the writer placed the characters of the story and then expressed their actions. The principle is as simple as advice about revising: When your prose—or anyone else's—feels turgid, abstract, too complex, do two things.

First, locate the cast of characters and the actions that those characters are performing (or are the objects of).

Then if you find that those characters don't appear in the subjects of their sentences, and that the actions those characters perform appear not in verbs but in abstract nouns, revise: Make your subjects name characters, and make your verbs name their actions.

In some cases, writers exclude characters altogether.

> The argument that failure to provide for reduction of the royalty rate upon expiration of the patent discourages challenges to the patent does not apply here.

The person who wrote this knew who was arguing, failing, reducing, and challenging, but his readers had to infer that knowledge from the context of the passage, a task that unnecessarily increases the readers' work. The writer would have saved his readers that extra work if he had named his cast of characters as the subjects of his verbs:

> Harris has argued that because Smith failed to provide him with a way to reduce the royalty rate when the patent expired, Smith discouraged him from challenging the patent. Harris is wrong.

There are other principles of good writing. But this first one carries us a long way—verbs for significant actions, characters as the subjects of those verbs.

SOME STYLISTIC CONSEQUENCES

We begin with this principle because it has so many consequences:

1. You may have been told to write specifically, concretely. When you turn verbs into nouns and delete the characters associated with those verbs, you fill a sentence with abstract nouns:

    > An affirmative decision has been reached in regard to termination of the program.

    When you use subjects to name characters and verbs to name their actions, you write sentences that are more specific and concrete.

    > Congress decided to terminate the program.

2. You may have been told not to use too many prepositional phrases.

While it is not clear what counts as "too many," it is clear that when you use specific verbs instead of their corresponding abstract nouns, you can eliminate those prepositional phrases. Compare:

There will be an evaluation of the program by us in order to achieve greater efficiency in the servicing of clients.

We will evaluate the program so that we can serve clients better.

3. You may have been told to put your ideas in a logical order. When you turn verbs into nouns and then chain them into strings of prepositional phrases, you can confuse the logical sequence of the actions:

Decisions in regard to the administration of medication despite the inability of irrational patients appearing in Trauma Centers to provide legal consent rest with the physician alone.

When you use subjects to name characters and verbs to name their actions, you are more likely to match your syntax to your logic:

When a patient appears in a Trauma Center and behaves so irrationally that he cannot legally consent to treatment, the physician alone must decide whether to administer medication.

4. You may have been told to use explicit connectors to make those logical relationships clear. When you turn nouns back into verbs, you have to use words like *because, although, if,* and *when,* to link the new sequences of clauses:

Presentation of more pressing needs by other interests resulted in our failure to acquire federal funds, despite intensive lobbying efforts.

Though we lobbied Congress intensively, we could not acquire federal funds **because** other interests presented more pressing needs.

In short, out of this first principle flow other important, but subordinate principles. Once you understand the root principle, you can apply it quickly, confident that as you solve one problem, you will be solving other problems as well.

VERBS AND ACTIONS

As we'll use the word here, *action* will cover not only physical movement but also mental processes, feelings, and relationships, concrete or abstract, literal or figurative. Compare the verbs in these pairs:

> There **will be** a suspension of the program by the dean until his reevaluation of it has been completed.

> The dean **will suspend** the program until he **has reevaluated** it.

> At the time of several Congressional committee investigations of the CIA, they **performed** no intelligence collection analysis.

> Several Congressional committees **investigated** the CIA, but they **did** not **analyze** how the CIA **collected** intelligence data.

Suspend and *reevaluate* are more specific than *be* and *occur. Investigate, collect,* and *analyze,* are more specific than *perform.*

In these next four sentences, the meaning becomes increasingly clear as the verbs become increasingly specific:

> There **has been** effective staff information dissemination control on the part of the secretary.

> The secretary **has exercised** effective staff information dissemination control.

> The secretary **has** effectively **controlled** staff information dissemination.

> The secretary **has** effectively **controlled** how the staff **disseminates** information.

The crucial actions aren't *be* or *exercise* but *control* and *disseminate.*

Most writers of turgid prose use verbs not to express actions but merely to state that those actions exist. In each of the wordier sentences below, the writer named significant actions and conditions in a noun derived from a verb or adjective. Their verbs merely assert that the action exists.

> A **need** *exists* for more efficient   =   We **must select** candidates
> candidate **selection.**   more efficiently.

There *is* the **possibility** of prior **approval** of it.	= He **may approve** of it ahead of time.
We *conducted* an **investigation** of it.	= We **investigated** it.
A **review** *was done* of the relevant regulations.	= They **reviewed** the relevant regulations.
We *had* a **discussion** of the matter.	= We **discussed** the matter.
The **establishment** of a different **approach** on the part of the committee *has become* a **necessity**.	= The committee **must approach** it differently.

When we turn a verb into a noun, we call that noun a **nominalization**. The term *nominalization* is itself a nominalization: *nominalize* > *nominalization*. We can nominalize not only verbs, but adjectives as well. Here are some examples:

Verb	> Nominalization	Adjective	> Nominalization
discover	discovery	careless	carelessness
move	movement	difficult	difficulty
resist	resistance	different	difference
react	reaction	elegant	elegance
impede	impedance	equal	equality
fail	failure	applicable	applicability
refuse	refusal	intense	intensity

Some nominalizations are identical to their corresponding verb:

hope	> *hope*	*charge*	> *charge*	*result*	> *result*
answer	> *answer*	*repair*	> *repair*	*return*	> *return*

Our *request* is that on your *return*, you conduct a *review* of the data and provide an immediate *report*.

We *request* that when you *return*, you *review* the data and *report* immediately.

As we'll see, we cannot express every action in a verb. Some nominalizations serve useful purposes. But those who write the clearest, the most direct and concise prose consistently use their verbs to express the crucial actions that constitute their story.

SUBJECTS AND CHARACTERS

Just as verbs and actions go together, so do subjects and characters. There are different kinds of characters. Usually—but not always—the most important characters are the Agents of actions, the source of the action or the condition that the writer is describing. The Agents include collective agents:

> *Faculties* of national eminence do not always teach well.

and figurative agents:

> *The White House* today announced the President's schedule.

> *The business sector* is cooperating.

> *Many instances of malignant tumors* fail to seek attention.

In some sentences, we use subjects to name things that are really the means, the instrument, by which some unstated agent performs its action, making the instrument seem like a metaphorical agent.

> *Studies* of coal production reveal these figures.

> *These data* establish the need for more detailed analysis.

> *This evidence* proves my theory.

In these sentences, the instruments are so much like agents that there is little point in revising them.

Some characters are difficult to locate. First, we saw how a writer can wholly depopulate a sentence:

> In the last sentence of the *Gettysburg Address* there is a rallying cry for the continuation of the struggle.

> In the last sentence of the *Gettysburg Address*, **Lincoln** rallies **his audience** to continue the struggle against **the South**.

In other sentences, the writer may imply a character in an adjective:

> Determination of policy occurs at the **presidential** level.

> The **President** determines policy.

Medieval **theological** debates often addressed what to **contemporary** thought seems to be metaphysical triviality.

Medieval **theologians** often debated issues that **we** might think were metaphysically trivial.

More often, the characters in abstract prose appear in words and phrases that modify the nominalization, or as objects in prepositional phrases beginning with *by, of, on the part of,* etc.

The **Federalists'** belief that the instability *of* **government** was a consequence *of* **popular democracy** was based on their belief in the tendency *on the part of* **factions** to further **their** self-interest at the expense of the common good.

The **Federalists** believed that **popular democracy** destabilized **government** because **they** believed that **factions** tended to further their self-interest at the expense of the common good.

The principle that characters should be subjects is not an exceptionless rule, only a reliable guide. Later we will see when we have to ignore this principle.

LOOKING FOR NOMINALIZATIONS

A few patterns of useless nominalization are easy to spot and revise.

1. When the nominalization follows an empty verb, change the nominalization to a verb that can replace the empty verb.

    The police **conducted** an *investigation* into the matter.

    The police **investigated** the matter.

    The committee **has** no *expectation* that it will meet the deadline.

    The committee does not **expect** to meet the deadline.

2. When the nominalization follows a *there is* or *there are,* change the nominalization to a verb and find a subject:

There is a *need* for further *study* of this program.

The engineering staff **must study** this program further.

There **was** considerable *erosion* of the land from the floods.

The floods considerably **eroded** the land.

3. When the nominalization is the subject of an empty verb, change the nominalization to a verb and find a new subject:

Our *intention* **is** to audit the records of the program.

We **intend** to audit the records of the program.

The *discussion* **concerned** a tax cut.

They **discussed** a tax cut.

4. When you find two nominalizations in a row, make at least the first into a verb. Then either leave the second as it is or turn it into a verb in a clause beginning with **how** or **why**.

There was first a **review** of the **evolution** of the dorsal fin.

First, she **reviewed** the **evolution** of the dorsal fin.

First, she **reviewed** *how* the dorsal fin **evolved**.

The mayor could offer no **explanation** for his **popularity decline**.

The mayor could not **explain** his **popularity decline**.

The mayor could not **explain** *why* his **popularity** had **declined**.

The mayor could not **explain** why he was less **popular**.

5. We have to revise most extensively when a nominalization in a subject is linked to another nominalization in the predicate:

Subject:	Their **cessation** of hostilities
Logical connection:	was because of
Object:	their personnel **losses**.

We revise such sentences like this:

(a) Change abstractions to verbs: *cessation* > *cease, loss* > *lose*
(b) Find subjects for those verbs: *they ceased, they lost.*
(c) Link the new clauses with a word that expresses their logical connection.

—To express cause: *because, since, when*
—To express condition: *if, provided, that*
—To express reservation: *though, although*

Schematically, we do this:

Their **cessation** of hostilities	⇒	they ceased hostilities
was because of	⇒	because
their personnel **losses**	⇒	they lost personnel

More examples:

The **discovery** of a method for the **manufacture** of artificial skin
will have the result of
a great increase in the **survival** of patients with radical burns.

—Researchers **discover** how to **manufacture** artificial skin
—More patients **will survive** radical burns. . . .

IF researchers **can discover** how to **manufacture** artificial skin, many
more patients **will survive** radical burns.

The presence of extensive rust **damage** to exterior surfaces
prevented
immediate **repairs** to the hull.

—Rust had extensively **damaged** the exterior surfaces. . . .
—We could not **repair** the hull immediately. . . .

BECAUSE rust had extensively **damaged** the exterior surfaces, we could
not **repair** the hull immediately.

The **instability** of the motor housing
did not preclude
the **completion** of the field trials.

—The motor housing was **unstable**. . . .
—The research staff **completed** field trials. . . .

EVEN THOUGH the motor housing was **unstable,** the research staff **completed** the field trials.

USEFUL NOMINALIZATIONS

In some cases, nominalizations are useful, even necessary. Don't bother trying to revise these.

1.   The nominalization is a subject that refers to a previous sentence:

These arguments all depend on a single unproven claim.

This decision can lead to costly consequences.

Such an agreement is in everyone's best interests.

These nominalizations let us link sentences into a more cohesive flow.

2.   The nominalization names what would be the object of its verb:

I do not understand either *her meaning* or *his intention.*

rather than the wordier:

I do not understand either *what she means* or *what he intends.*

We don't improve these much by changing nominalizations into clauses.

3.   A succinct nominalization can replace an awkward *The fact that:*

The fact that I denied what he accused me of impressed the jury.

My denial of his accusations impressed the jury.

But then why not

When I *denied* his accusations, I impressed the jury.

4.   Some nominalizations refer to an often repeated concept.

Few issues have so divided Americans as *abortion* on *demand.*

> The Equal Rights *Amendment* was an issue in past *elections*.

> *Taxation* without *representation* was not the central concern of the American *Revolution*.

In each of those sentences, the nominalization names ideas that we refer to over and over: *abortion on demand, Amendment, election, taxation, representation, Revolution.* Rather than repeatedly spell out a familiar concept in a full clause, we contract it into a concise noun. In these cases, the abstractions become virtual actors.

And, of course, some nominalizations name ideas that we can express only in nominalizations: *freedom, death, love, hope, life, wisdom.* If we couldn't turn some verbs or adjectives into nouns, we would find it difficult—perhaps impossible—to discuss those subjects that have preoccupied us for millennia. You simply have to develop an eye—or an ear—for the nominalization that expresses one of these ideas and the nominalization that hides a significant action:

> There is a **demand** for an **end** to **taxation** on **entertainment**.

> We *demand* that the government no longer *tax* entertainment.

Exercise 2-1

Rewrite these sentences in a more direct style. In 1–5, both agents and actions are in italics. State the agents as subjects and the actions or conditions as verbs or adjectives.

1.   *Our expectation* was to establish new tolerance levels.
2.   *Attempts* were made on the part of the *engineering staff* in regard to an *assessment* of the project.
3.   There were *expectations* by the *governing committee* that *their* report *submission* would meet the deadline.
4.   The *appearance* of the *candidate* before the board was on May 30.
5.   *The governor's refusal* of the request is a *necessity*.

In sentences 6–10, only the agents are in italics.

6.   A *presidential* appeal was made to *the American people* for the conservation of gasoline.
7.   More accurate measurements of the thorium half-life were conducted at that time by *independent investigators*.

8. Discussions by the *participants* of the future of the program were conducted amicably.

9. There was no independent *business-sector analysis* of the cause of the trade deficit.

10. Agreement as to the need for revisions in the terms of the treaty was reached by *the two sides*.

In 11–15, only the nominalizations are in italics.

11. There was *uneasiness* among management over the survey.

12. There must be thorough *preparation* of the specimen sections by the laboratory personnel.

13. The discrepancy in the data demands *checking* by the insurer.

14. The *rejection* of the application by the dean was unexpected.

15. The performance by the police of an *investigation* into the affair occurred without delay.

In the next ten items, neither agent nor action is identified. Where necessary, invent agents.

16. There should be no hesitation in regard to saying no.

17. The same principles of bilateral symmetry received study after the last report.

18. A solution to the problem of UFOs will never be found by the Air Force.

19. It is my belief that there should be consultation by the administrators with the student body before changes in rules are made.

20. Cutbacks in loan availability are mandated as a result of lack of success in the acquisition of federal funding.

21. A redetermination of their personnel needs is necessary before assistance from local sources can be provided.

22. With the decline in enrollments in undergraduate and graduate literature courses, there seems to be a growing awareness, among faculty members in the department of English and university administrators, of the importance of the contribution of the writing program and a corresponding disposition toward the recognition and reward of those who provide this valuable service for the students at the University.

23. The President's recent assertion in regard to the chronic inability of the press to present information accurately and fairly is an insightful description of press reporting in the Middle East today. Indeed a comparison of the coverage of different events in the region will reveal the inaccuracies of American journalists, particularly those

associated with certain politically biased newspapers. The omission of facts, the exaggeration of local conflicts, the slanting of stories all show the failure of the press to carry out its mission with the independence expected of American newspaper reporters. As a consequence, a lack of accurate knowledge of the events of the area has resulted in the formation of American public opinion more on the basis of emotion than of reason.

24. In regard to your reporting about the effects of your petroleum production facilities on the environment, it is our opinion that despite the Environmental Protection Agency's retention of its earlier regulations, there has been a modification in its policy. There is a greater emphasis placed on the requirement that companies such as yours provide continuing accurate estimates as to the effect of any new facilities on the environment, if it appears that the amounts of your petroleum products might be considered significant by the EPA. At the present time, however, these adjustments in its approach do not yet seem to require any new studies of these effects. A review of older studies already performed may be sufficient for a determination of their applicability to your present situation.

PASSIVES AND AGENTS

You will usually make your style more vigorous and direct if, in addition to avoiding abstract nominalizations, you also avoid unnecessary passive verbs. In active sentences, the subject typically expresses the Agent of an action, and the object expresses the goal or the thing changed by the action:

	subject			object
Active:	The partners	⇒	broke ⇒	the agreement.
	agent			goal

In passive sentences, the subject expresses the goal of an action; a form of *be* always precedes a past participle form of the verb; and the Agent of the action may appear in a *by*-phrase:

	subject			prepositional phrase
Passive:	The agreement	⇐	was broken ⇐	(by the partners).
	goal			agent

We almost always make our style more vigorous and more direct if we avoid both nominalizations and **unnecessary** passive verbs. Compare:

A new method for the decomposition of toxic by-products of refinery processes *has been discovered* by Genco Chemical. Estimates of savings of up to 40% of recovery costs *have been made* but no details of the process *have been released.*

First change the passives to actives:

Genco Chemical has discovered a new method for the **decomposition** of toxic by-products of refinery processes. Genco has made **estimates** of **savings** of up to 40% of recovery costs but has not yet released any details of the process.

Then change the nominalizations back to verbs:

Genco Chemical has discovered a new method to **decompose** toxic by-products of refinery processes. It has **estimated** that refineries will **save** up to 40% of recovery costs but has released no details of the process.

Writing an active sentence encourages us to name the specific agent of an action and lets us avoid a few extra words—a form of *be* and, when we keep the Agent of the action in the sentence, the preposition *by*. Because the passive also reverses the more direct order of agent-action-goal, passives eventually cripple the easy flow of an otherwise energetic style. Compare these passages:

It *was found* that data concerning energy resources allocated to the states *were not obtained.* This action *is needed* so that a determination of redirection *is permitted* on a timely basis when weather conditions change. A system *must be established* so that data on weather conditions and fuel consumption *may be gathered* on a regular basis.

We *found* that the Department of Energy *did not obtain* data about energy resources that Federal offices *were allocating* to the states. The Department *needs* these data so that it *can determine* how to *redirect* these resources when conditions *change.* The Secretary of the Department *must establish* a system so that his office *can gather* data on weather conditions and fuel consumption on a regular basis.

The second passage is a bit longer, but more specific and more straightforward. We know who is supposed to be doing what.

When we combine passives with nominalizations, we create that wretched prose we call legalese, sociologese, educationese, bureaucratese—

all of the *-eses* of those who confuse authority and objectivity with polysyllabic abstraction and remote impersonality:

> Patient movement to less restrictive methods of care may be followed by increased probability of recovery.

> If we treat patients less restrictively, they may recover faster.

But those are the easy generalizations. In many other cases, we may find that the passive is, in fact, the better choice.

CHOOSING BETWEEN ACTIVE AND PASSIVE

To choose between the active and the passive, we have to answer three questions: First, must our audience know who is performing the action? Second, are we maintaining a logically consistent string of subjects? And third, if the string of subjects is consistent, is it the right string of subjects?

Often, we don't say who is responsible for an action, because we don't know or don't care, or because we'd just rather not say:

> Between July 2 and July 9, over 5,000 brochures *were printed.*

> If a person *is found* guilty of negligence, he or she *can be sued.*

> Valuable records *should always be kept* in a fireproof safe.

In sentences like these, the passive is the natural and correct choice.

In this next sentence, the passive might be the predictable choice, but for a different reason:

> Because the final safety inspection, *was* neither *performed* nor *monitored,* the brake plate assembly mechanism *was left* incorrectly aligned, information that *was known* several months before it *was decided* to publicly *reveal* that information.

In this case, we might wonder whether the writer explicitly decided not to name names and so chose the passive. But that is a question which raises issues more significant than mere clarity.

There is a second consideration in choosing between the active and passive. It is whether active verbs or passive verbs will allow the writer to create a sequence of sentences with subjects that the reader will feel are consistent, logically related. Look again at the subjects in the pair of paragraphs about energy data (p. 23). In the first version the subjects of the passive sentences seem to be chosen almost at random:

> It . . . data concerning energy resources allocated to the states. . . . This action . . . a determination of redirection, . . . A system . . . data on weather conditions and fuel consumption.

In the revised passage, the active verbs give the reader a consistent point of view; the writer "stages" the sentences from a consistent string of subjects, in this case the Agents of the Action.

> We. . . . Department of Energy. . . . Federal offices. . . . The Department . . . it. . . . The Secretary . . . his office. . . .

In the revised passage the subject of every sentence and even every subordinate clause anchors the reader in something familiar—the cast of characters, the agents of the actions, before the reader moves on to something new.

If in a series of passive sentences, you find yourself constantly shifting from one unrelated subject to another, try rewriting those sentences in the active. Use the beginning of your sentence to orient your reader to what follows. If in a series of sentences you give your reader no consistent starting point, the passage may well seem disjointed, out of focus.

On the other hand, if you can make a consistent series of subjects out of characters who are **not** the agents of actions but the goals of someone else's action, then do not hesitate to choose the passive, so long as (1) the reader knows who that someone else is or (2) it doesn't matter who acts. In this next passage, the writer wanted to write about the end of WWII from the point of view of Germany and Japan. So in each of her sentences, she put Germany and Japan into the subject of a verb, regardless of whether the verb was active or passive:

> By March of 1945, the world knew that *The Axis nations* had been defeated, that all that remained was a final but bloody climax. *The borders of Germany* had been breached, and *both Germany and Japan* were being bombed around the clock. *Neither country,* though, had been so devastated that *it* could not exact a terrible final price on the Allied forces in their final push.

If she had wanted to write about the end of WWII from the point of view of the Allied nations, the active would have been the better choice.

> By March of 1945, the world knew that *the Allies* had defeated the Axis nations, that all that remained was a final but bloody climax. *American, French, and British forces* had breached the borders of Germany, *the allied air forces* were bombing Germany around the clock, and *the American airforce* was reducing Japan to ruins. But *the Allies* had not so devastated either country that *they* would not have to pay a terrible price in their final push.

We will return to this question in Lesson Three.

THE INSTITUTIONAL PASSIVE

Nowhere is the passive more predictable than in prose that appears in academic or bureaucratic publications. We'll call that kind of passive "the institutional passive" not only because it is used in institutions, but because it has become institutionalized as part of that style. Here is an example:

> On the basis of their verbal intelligence, prior knowledge and essay scores (the essays *were analyzed* for hierarchical structure and *were evaluated* according to the richness of concepts), the subjects *were subdivided* into a high- or low ability group. Half of each group *was* then randomly *assigned* to a treatment or a placebo group. A separate analysis *was done* on the learners' self-efficacy ratings.

When we try to revise passives in institutional prose, we often run into a problem, because many editors and teachers of such writing will not accept prose written in first person *I* or *we*.

In fact, many writers of academic prose use the first person quite regularly. These passages come from the openings of articles published in very respectable journals:

> This paper is concerned with two problems. How can **we** best handle, in a transformational grammar (i) Restrictions. . . . To illustrate (i), **we** may cite . . . **we** shall show. . . .

> Since the pituitary-adrenal axis is activated during the acute phase response, **we** have investigated the potential role. . . . Specifically, **we** have studied the effects of interleukin-1. . . .

Any study of tensions presupposes some acquaintance with certain findings of child psychology. **We** may begin by inquiring whether . . . **we**
should next proceed to investigate.

Here are the first few words from several consecutive sentences in an
article in *Science,* a journal of considerable prestige:

. . . **we** want. . . . Survival gives. . . . **We** examine. . . . **We** compare. .
. .

. . . **We** have used. . . . Each has been weighted. . . . **We** merely take.
. . . They are subject. . . . **We** use. . . . Efron and Morris (3) describe.
. . . **We** observed. . . . **We** might find. . . . **We** know. . . . Averages
for a season ordinarily run. . . . Spread comes. . . . **We** can shrink.
. . . How this is done is explained. . . .
   —John P. Gilbert, Bucknam McPeek, and Frederick Mosteller,
   "Statistics and Ethics in Surgery and Anesthesia," *Science*

Now, to be sure, we cannot claim that all scholars in all fields write
the same way. Some scholarly writers and some editors resolutely avoid the
first person everywhere. But we can be certain of one thing: Those who
claim that good academic writing is always impersonally third-person,
always passive, are wrong.

METADISCOURSE: WRITING ABOUT WRITING

When academic and scholarly writers do use the first person, though, they
do not use it randomly, but in particular ways. Look at these verbs in the
passages cited: *cite, show, begin by inquiring, next proceed to investigate,
compare.* With those words the writers are referring not to what they are
principally writing about—statistics, ethics, grammar, child psychology—
but reflexively, to their own processes of writing or arguing, or to how they
feel or think about their subject:

We **believe** that these particular observations **could be** an artifact of
observer bias. Fortunately, other data are available.

The writers are using what we shall call **metadiscourse.**
   Metadiscourse is the language that we use when we describe what we
are doing as we think and write about the content of our primary ideas, or
what we want our readers to be doing as they read. It is writing about

reading and writing. When we communicate, we use metadiscourse to name rhetorical actions: *explain, show, argue, claim, deny, describe, suggest, contrast, add, expand, summarize;* to name the parts of our discourse: *first, second, third; to begin, in conclusion;* to reveal logical connections: *therefore, however, on the other hand, if so;* to hedge our beliefs: *it seems that, perhaps, I believe;* to guide our readers: *Consider now the matter of, . . . We might at this point recall.*

Metadiscourse does not refer directly to our primary topic, but we still need some metadiscourse in everything we write because it helps us manage how readers understand us.

If academic writers use the first person at all, they will typically use *I* or *we* in metadiscourse in introductions, where they announce their intentions: *We claim that. . . , We shall show. . . , We begin by examining. . . .* If they use metadiscourse at the beginning, they may very likely use it again at the end, when they summarize what they have done: *We have suggested. . . , I have shown that. . . , We have, however, not claimed. . . .* Regardless of where the metadiscourse occurs, however—beginning, middle, or end— substantial numbers of entirely competent writers in all fields use metadiscourse in the first person. Others avoid the first person, for reasons of modesty, inappropriateness, or sheer habit. For obvious reasons, joint authors are more likely to use *we* than a single author will use *I.* It is all a matter of choice. (Of course, if you are writing under someone else's supervision and that person has strong opinions on the matter, then it's that person's choice).

Somewhat less often, scholarly writers use the first person to name the general actions they performed when they researched their problem: *we can investigate, study, examine, know, analyze, review, evaluate, assess, find, discover*—words that refer to generic actions that constitute research.

On the other hand, academic and scholarly writers rarely use the first person to describe **particular** actions they performed. We are unlikely to find passages such as this:

> To determine if monokines directly elicited an adrenal steroidogenic response, I added monocyte-conditioned medium and purified preparations of . . .

Far more likely is the original sentence:

> To determine if monokines directly elicited an adrenal steroidogenic response, **monocyte-conditioned medium and purified preparations of** . . . were added to cultures of . . .

When the writer put that sentence in the passive, he quite unself-consciously dangled his modifier:

> To determine if. . . , . . . medium and purified preparations were added to
> . . .

The implied subject of the infinitive verb *determine* is I or we: *I determine*. But that implied subject I or we differs from the explicit subject of the main verb, *medium and purified preparations*. That's what dangles a modifier: The implied subject of the introductory phrase differs from the explicit subject of the main clause.

Writers of scientific prose use this particular pattern so often that it has become standard in most academic writing. The few editors who take a stern view of this matter object, of course. But if they do, they must then accept first person subjects. If they both deprive their authors of the first person and rule out dangling modifiers, they put their authors into a damned-if-you-do, damned-if-you-don't predicament.

As a small historical footnote, we might note that this impersonal "scientific" style is a modern development. In his "New Theory of Light and Colors" (1672), Sir Isaac Newton wrote this rather charming account of an early experiment:

> I procured a triangular glass prism, to try therewith the celebrated phenomena of colors. And for that purpose, having darkened my laboratory, and made a small hole in my window shade, to let in a convenient quantity of the sun's light, I placed my prism at the entrance, that the light might be thereby refracted to the opposite wall. It was at first a very pleasing diversion to view the vivid and intense colors produced thereby.

THE PROFESSIONAL VOICE

It is true that every profession—any group, professional or not—demands of its members a tone of voice and vocabulary that testify a writer has accepted the implicit values that define the group. A physicist, or engineer, or psychologist must learn not only to think like a professional, but also to sound like one as well. To be sure, even if scholars always wrote clearly, we still would find much of their writing difficult. To understand advanced work in any field requires that we possess the knowledge known only to its inhabitants, that we control their technical vocabulary and understand the nuances of their particular forms of argument.

But when an unfriendly prose style conspires with problems of substantive complexity, it becomes difficult, if not impossible, for the educated lay-person to appreciate even the outlines of issues that may have significant consequences for society in general. Some claim that high-level scholarship cannot be made clear to the lay-reader. Sometimes, perhaps, but less often than a lot of scholars might think. Here, for example, is an excerpt from an article by Talcott Parsons, a social scientist who was as influential in shaping the way sociologists think about society as he was notorious for his opaque style.

> Apart from theoretical conceptualization there would appear to be no method of selecting among the indefinite number of varying kinds of factual observation which can be made about a concrete phenomenon or field so that the various descriptive statements about it articulate into a coherent whole, which constitutes an "adequate," a "determinate" description. Adequacy in description is secured in so far as determinate and verifiable answers can be given to all the scientifically important questions involved. What questions are important is largely determined by the logical structure of the generalized conceptual scheme which, implicitly or explicitly, is employed.

If we revise this passage in all the ways we've described, we can make it accessible to a moderately well-educated audience:

> If scientists have no theory, they have no way to select from among everything they could say about something only that which would fit into a coherent whole, a whole that would be "adequate" or "determinate." Scientists describe something "adequately" only when they can verify answers to questions that they think are important. They decide what questions are important on the basis of the theories that they implicitly or explicitly use.

And even that could be made more direct:

> To describe something so that you can fit it into a whole, you need a theory. When you ask a question, you need a theory to verify your answer. Your theory even determines your question.

The simplest version may omit some of the nuances. But Parson's excruciating style must numb all but his most masochistically dedicated readers.

Exercise 2-2

Revise these passages. Change passives into actives only where doing so will improve the sentence. If necessary, invent a rhetorical situation to account for your choice of active or passive.

1.   Your figures have been reanalyzed in order to determine the coefficient of error. The results will be announced when the situation is judged appropriate.
2.   Almost all home mortgage loans nowadays are made for twenty-five years. With the price of housing at such inflated levels, those loans cannot be paid off in any shorter period of time.
3.   Trotsky's usual impassioned narrative style is abandoned and in its place a cautious and scholarly treatment of theories of conspiracy is presented. But the moment the narrative line is picked up again, he invests his prose with the same vigor and force.
4.   Many arguments have been advanced against Darwinian evolution because basic assumptions about our place in the world were contradicted by it. No longer was man seen as the privileged creature in God's Great Scheme of Things but rather as an accidental consequence of natural forces.
5.   For many years federal regulations concerning the use of wiretapping have been regularly ignored. Only recently have tighter restrictions been imposed on the circumstances that warrant it.

In these next sentences, change passives to actives and edit nominalizations into a more direct agent-action style. Again, invent agents where necessary.

6.   It is my belief that the social significance of Restoration comedy can be provided with the clearest explanation through an analysis of social relationships portrayed in the plays. In particular, studies can be made of the manner in which interactions between different social levels are conducted.

7. These technical directives are written in a style of maximum simplicity as a result of an attempt at more effective communication with employees of little education who have been hired in accordance with guidelines that have been imposed.

8. The participants received information that they would be reimbursed, but a decision has been made that such an action cannot be accomplished at this time.

9. The tissue rejection evaluation was performed according to procedures that have been abandoned because of their consistent overestimation of antibody production values.

10. The ability of the human brain to arrive at solutions of human problems has been undervalued, because research has not been done that would be considered to have scientific reliability.

11. To search for completeness and fairness in analyzing how the process of schooling is linked to cultivation of reasoning will frame the problem of school reform most accurately.

12. [This next is a passage in which some nominalizations refer to technical concepts, terms that we would not convert into verbs because if we did, we would lose the technical meaning. One of those terms is *class consciousness*. Another is *socio-economic planning*. There may be others. So as you work through this passage, be conscious of the fact that you will not be able to revise every nominalization back into a verbal phrase.]

The possibility of the development of class-consciousness among the middle class depends on the synthesis of the ideologies of the dominant class and working class in their struggle for middle class support. Predictions of any degree of certainty in regard to the form which this emergent class consciousness may take are at best difficult, but an historical analysis of the ideological struggle would indicate that among its primary components would be included elements derived from both the bourgeois-libertarian tradition and the developing working class program from the reconstruction of society through collective action and the socialization of production. An adequate middle class ideology would appear therefore to involve a middle class recognition of the necessity of achieving a reconciliation of the need for adequate socio-economic planning with the traditional guarantees of civil rights which best can be maintained through the relative political independence of such groups as the press, the university, and the trade unions.

13.

The absence from this dictionary of a handful of old, well-known vulgate terms for sexual and excretory organs and functions is not due to a lack of citations for these words from current literature. On the contrary, the profusion of such citations in recent years would suggest that the terms in question are so well known as to require no explanation. The decision to eliminate them as part of the extensive culling process that is the inevitable task of the lexicographer was made on the practical grounds that there is still objection in many quarters to the appearance of these terms in print and that to risk keeping this dictionary out of the hands of some students by introducing several terms that require little if any elucidation would be unwise.

from "Foreword," *Webster's New World Dictionary of the American Language,* 1980

NOUN + NOUN + NOUN

A last point of style that often keeps us from being as clear and as direct as we might is the long compound noun phrase.

Early childhood thought disorder misdiagnosis often occurs as a result of unfamiliarity with recent *research literature* describing such conditions. This paper is a review of seven recent studies in which are findings of particular relevance to *preteen hyperactivity diagnosis* and to *treatment modalities* involving *medication maintenance level evaluation procedures.*

Some grammarians insist that one noun should never modify another, but that would rule out such common phrases as *stone wall, student committee,* or *radio telescope.* We can more persuasively reject long series of nouns used as adjectives on the grounds that most of them are awkward, or worse, ambiguous, especially when they include nominalizations. Their slight economy may sometimes be a bad bargain.

Whenever you find a string of nouns that you haven't seen before, try dis-assembling them. Start from the last and reverse their order, linking them with prepositional phrases. If one of the nouns is a nominalization, rewrite it into a full verb. Here is the first compound in the example passage revised:

<pre>
         1   2   3   4
early childhood thought disorder misdiagnosis
         4   3   2   1
⇒ misdiagnosis disordered thought in early childhood
</pre>

(Now we can see an ambiguity: What's early, the childhood, the disorder, or the diagnosis?) Now just re-assemble into a sentence:

> Physicians are misdiagnosing disordered thought in young children because they are not familiar with the literature on recent research.

Exercise 2-3

Turn the compound noun phrases in 1-5 into prepositional phrases.

1. The plant safety standards committee discussed recent air quality regulation announcements.
2. Diabetic patient blood pressure reduction may be a consequence of renal extract depressor agent application.
3. Pancreatic gland motor phenomena are regulated chiefly by parasympathetic nervous system cells.
4. The main goal of this article is to describe text comprehension processes and recall protocol production.
5. On the basis of these principles, we may now attempt to formulate narrative information extraction rules.

In these next sentences, unpack compound nouns, and edit the indirect style by placing agents and actions in subjects and verbs. Invent agents where necessary.

6. This paper is an investigation into information processing behavior involved in computer human cognition simulation games.
7. Enforcement of guidelines for new car model tire durability is a Federal Trade Commission responsibility.
8. Upon court appearance by the defendant, courtroom legal service will be effected by the presiding justice with the request for time requirement waiver so that the case hearing can begin.
9. The Social Security program is a standard monthly income floor guarantee for individuals whose benefit package potential is based on a determination of lifelong contribution schedule.

10. Based on extensive training needs assessment reviews and on selected PIC office site visits, there was the identification of concepts and issues to constitute an initial staff questionnaire instrument.

11. Corporation organization under state law supervision has resulted in federal government inability as to effective implementation of pollution reduction measures.

12. Determination of support appropriateness for community organization assistance need was precluded by difficulty in the obtaining of data relevant to a committee activity review.

13. The secretary of the Department of Energy's November 1, 1989, press release announcement was to the effect that there was a decision for surplus alcohol stock disposal on the part of major manufacturers as a result of the October 28 meeting discussions between the manufacturers and the DOE.

14. The existence of these aforementioned conditions in regard to improper reimbursement claims is due to compliance failure of relevant school personnel and to student reimbursement claim reviews being ineffective or inadequate.

15. The art of cardiac sound interpretation requires an intimate cardiac physiology and cardiac disease pathophysiology knowledge.

SUMMING UP

1. Whenever you can, express actions and conditions in specific verbs, adverbs, or adjectives:

   The **intention** of the committee is the **improvement** of morale.

   The committee **intends** to **improve** morale.

2. When it is appropriate, make the subjects of your verbs the agents of those actions.

   A decision on the part of **the Dean** in regard to the funding by **the Department** of the program must be made for there to be adequate **staff** preparation.

   If **the staff** is to prepare adequately, **the Dean** must decide whether **the Department** will fund the program.

3. Do not revise passives into actives if the agent of the action is unknown or unimportant:

   The President **was reelected** with 54% of the vote.

4. Do not rewrite into verbs those nominalizations that sum up in a subject what went before or that refer to a well-established concept:

   Analyses of this kind invariably produce misleading results.

   Dose response variables include type of *medication* and its **absorption** rates.

   We can sum up all these principles into this tidy scheme:

subject	verb	
cast of characters	action	

   This, however, is only the first step toward clear, direct, and **coherent** writing.

The Grammar of Cohesion

Well begun is half done.
ANONYMOUS

The two capital secrets in the art of prose composition are these: first the philosophy of transition and connection; or the art by which one step in an evolution of thought is made to arise out of another: all fluent and effective composition depends on the connections; secondly, the way in which sentences are made to modify each other; for the most powerful effects in written eloquence arise out of this reverberation, as it were, from each other in a rapid succession of sentences.
THOMAS DE QUINCEY

"Begin at the beginning," the King said, gravely, "and go on till you come to the end; then stop."
LEWIS CARROLL

CLARITY AND CONTEXT

S o far, we've talked about clear and direct writing as if we wrote only individual sentences, independent of any larger context or governing intention, as if we could just map our sentences onto the way agents and actions seem to behave in the world. And it's true, that if we arrange whatever agents and actions we think we are writing about so that they match subjects and verbs, we will achieve a kind of local clarity.

But there is more to good writing than local clarity. We can still mislead or confuse our readers if we fail to design those locally clear sentences to emphasize our most important ideas, if we fail to arrange the information in those sentences to fit its context. Furthermore, since almost all stories involve more than one character, we can almost always **choose** the character that we want to make the seeming agent of an action:

> Congress finally believed the Secretary of State that if the United States allied with Saudi Arabia, Kuwait might require American protection if it became an object of Iranian attack.

> The Secretary of State finally convinced Congress that the United States might have to protect Kuwait if Saudi Arabia allied itself with the United States and Iran attacked Kuwait.

> The Secretary of State finally convinced Congress that if the United States allied itself with Saudi Arabia and Iran then attacked Kuwait, the United States might have to protect Kuwait.

The problem is to discover how, without sacrificing clarity, we can shape sentences that are appropriate to their context and to those larger intentions that motivate us to write in the first place.

OLD AND NEW INFORMATION

Few principles of style are more widely repeated than "Use the direct active voice, avoid the weak and indirect passive." Not,

> (2a) A black hole *is created* by the collapse of a dead star into a point perhaps no larger than a marble.

but instead

> (2b) The collapse of a dead star into a point perhaps no larger than a
> marble *creates* a black hole.

But suppose the context for either of those sentences was this:

> (1) Some astonishing questions about the nature of the universe have
> been raised by scientists exploring the nature of black holes in space.
> (2a/b) _____ (3) So much matter compressed into so little volume
> changes the fabric of space around it in profoundly puzzling ways.

Our sense of coherence should tell us that this context calls not for
the active sentence, but for the passive. And the reasons are not far to seek:
The last part of sentence (1) introduces one of the important characters in
the story, . . . *black holes in space.* If we write sentence (2) in the active
voice, we cannot mention black holes again until the end as the object of an
active verb:

> (2b) The collapse of a dead star . . . *creates* a black hole.

We improve the flow between sentences (1) and (2) if we shift that
object in sentence (2)—*black hole*—to the beginning of its own sentence.
If we do that, then we put those repeated words closer to the same words at
the end of sentence (1). We do that by making *black hole* the subject of a
passive verb:

> (1) . . . the nature of *black holes in space.* (2a) *A black hole* is created by
> the collapse of a dead star (*or . . .* when a dead star collapses). . . .

By doing that, we also move to the end of sentence (2) the idea that will
open sentence (3):

> (1) . . . the nature of black holes in space. (2a) A black hole is created by
> the collapse of a dead star into *a point perhaps no larger than a marble.*
> (3) *So much matter compressed into so little volume* changes the fabric of
> space. . . .

The problem—and the challenge—of English prose is that every sentence
requires us to find the best compromise between the principles of clarity
and directness that we discussed in the second lesson and those principles
of cohesion that fuse separate sentences into a whole discourse. **But in**

making that compromise, we must always give priority to cohesion, to what fuses sentences into cohesive discourse.

We've just illustrated two complementary principles of order and emphasis. One of them is this.

> Put at the beginning of a sentence ideas that you have already stated, referred to, implied; ideas that you can safely assume your reader is familiar with, will readily recognize.

The other principle is this:

> Put at the end of your sentence the newest, the most surprising, the most significant information, information you want to stress, perhaps the information that you will expand on in the following sentence.

As you begin a sentence, you must prepare your readers for new and therefore important information. Give your readers a familiar context to help them move from the more familiar to the less familiar, from the known to the unknown.

BEGINNING WELL

It's harder to begin a sentence well than to end it well. As we'll see, to end a sentence well, we need only decide which idea is the newest, the most important, and then imagine that idea at the end of its sentence. The problem is to get there gracefully. Every time we begin a sentence, we may have to juggle three or four elements that typically occur early on:

1. To connect a sentence to the preceding one, we use transitional metadiscourse, such as *and, but, therefore, as a result.*
2. To help our readers understand how to evaluate what follows we use expressions such as *fortunately, perhaps, allegedly, it is important to note that, for the most part, in many ways, under these circumstances, to a certain extent, from a practical point of view, politically speaking.*
3. We typically set an action in time and place: *at that time, later, on May 23, in Europe.*
4. And most importantly (note the evaluation), we announce the *Topic* of a sentence. The Topic of a sentence is that concept named at the beginning that we intend to say something about. We either

name the Topic in the subject of a clause or we introduce it with phrases such as *in regard to, as for, turning now to, as far as X is concerned.*

Your style will be cohesive to the degree that you can subordinate the first three of these elements to the fourth. Because Topics are so important, we'll begin with them.

Topics: Psychological Subjects

Your most important concern at the beginning of a **series** of sentences should be their Topics. The Topic of a sentence is its **psychological** subject. The psychological subject of a sentence is that idea close to its beginning— almost always a noun phrase of some kind—that the rest of the sentence characterizes, comments on, says something about. In most English sentences, these psychological subjects, these Topics, are also grammatical subjects:

> *Private higher education* is seriously concerned about population trends through the end of the century.

The writer put out on the table first, in the grammatical subject, *Private higher education.* As readers, we assume the writer is going to characterize, comment on, say something about that concept. In that sense, the sentence is "about" *Private higher education.*

But we can also create a Topic out of the object of a verb if we shift that object to the beginning of its sentence, before the subject:

> I cannot explain *the reasons for this decision to end the treaty.*

> *The reasons for this decision to end the treaty* I cannot explain.

We can also put Topics in introductory phrases:

> As for *abortion,* it is not clear how the Court will rule.

> In regard to regulating *religious cults,* we must proceed cautiously.

Neither *abortion* nor *religious cults* is the subject of its sentence. The subject of the first is *it,* and of the second, *we.* If we ask what either of those sentences is "about," we would not say that the sentences were "about" their grammatical subjects, *it* or *we.* Those sentences are "about" their psychological subjects, their Topics—*abortion* and *religious cults.*

In the clearest writing, the Topics of most sentences—and of their subordinate clauses—are their subjects. But what's more important than defining their grammatical function is recognizing the crucial role they play in how we read.

The Role of Topics

Italics mark Topics in this paragraph:

> *Particular ideas toward the beginning of each clause* focus the reader's attention, so *Topics* are crucial. Cumulatively, *the thematic signposts that are provided by these ideas* should focus the reader's attention toward a well-defined set of connected ideas. *Moving through a paragraph from a cumulatively coherent point of view* is made possible by a sequence of Topics that seem to constitute a coherent sequence of connected ideas. *A lack of context for each sentence* is one consequence of making the reader begin sentences with random shifts in Topics. *Feelings of dislocation, disorientation, and lack of focus* will occur in the reader when *that* happens. *The rest of the sentence as well as whole paragraphs* will be affected by a reader's point of view as a result of Topic announcement.

If you found that paragraph disjointed, confusing, out of focus, compare it with this one in which the Topics of every clause are italicized:

> *Topics* are crucial because toward the beginning of each clause, *they* focus a reader's attention on a particular idea. Cumulatively, through a series of sentences, *these ideas* provide thematic signposts that should focus your reader's attention on a well-defined set of connected ideas. If *a sequence of Topics* seems coherent, *that consistent sequence* will move your reader through a paragraph from a cumulatively coherent point of view. But if through that paragraph *your Topics* shift randomly, then *your reader* has to begin each sentence out of context, from no coherent point of view. When *that* happens, *your reader* will feel dislocated, disoriented, out of focus. *You* must provide your readers with a coherent point of view, with a logical continuity that will guide them not only through individual sentences but through whole paragraphs.

Compare the sequences of Topics:

Original	**Revised**
Particular ideas toward the beginning of each clause	Topics

Topics	they (Topics)
the thematic signposts . . . by these ideas	these ideas
Moving through a paragraph from a cumulatively coherent point of view	a sequence of Topics that consistent sequence
A lack of context for each sentence	your Topics
	your reader
Feelings of dislocation, disorientation. . . .	that
	your reader
that	
The rest of the sentence . . . chunks of discourse	you

The original version has no consistent focus, no consistent string of Topics. So as we read it, we feel dislocated, disoriented, unfocused. The revised version consistently focuses on only two Topics: *Topics* and *reader*. It has a consistent string of Topics. This principle of a coherent Topic string also helps us understand why we are confused by one long sentence after another. Very long sentences don't announce Topics often enough or clearly enough to guide us through a multitude of ideas. We need thematic signposts to help our readers assemble ideas in individual sentences and clauses into cohesive discourse.

This principle reinforces the point we made about characters and actions: When you design your sentences so that their subjects predictably name your central characters—real or abstract—and the verbs in those sentences name crucial actions, you are beginning your sentences from a consistent point of view, from the point of view of your characters. As we are going to see, all the principles of clear writing fit together like this into a coherent *system* of principles, one principle reinforcing another.

Keeping Topics Visible

We might now appreciate why it is important to get a sentence off to a brisk start with the appropriate Topic. One way we hide Topics is to introduce sentences with metadiscourse, that language we use when we write about our own writing or thinking. Too much metadiscourse makes your reader work too hard to find those signals that provide the structural backbone to paragraphs—the string of Topics in a series of sentences. These next sentences appeared in a study of a college curriculum. They are typical of its author's style. I have bold-faced what I believe should have been the Topics.

We think it useful to provide some relatively detailed illustration of the varied ways "corporate curricular personalities" organize themselves in **programs.** *We choose to feature as a central device in our presentation what are called* introductory', 'survey', or 'foundational' courses.

i.e., **Programs** create varied "corporate" curricular personalities, particularly through their introductory', 'survey', or 'foundational' courses.

Yet once this is said, it is important to recognize the diversity of what occurs in **programs** after the different initial survey courses.

i.e., But after the initial survey courses, **programs** offer diverse curricula.

But what is also suggested is that if one talks about a **program** *simply in terms of* the intellectual strategies or techniques engaged in, *when* these *are understood in a general way,* it becomes difficult to distinguish many programs from others.

i.e., But **Many programs** employ almost identical intellectual strategies.

(The report in which these sentences appeared was in fact quite good. But it was largely ignored because so few of the writer's colleagues would willingly slog through 103 pages of this sort of prose.)

At this point, some of you may recall advice that you once received about how to avoid "monotony"—vary how you begin your sentences, avoid beginning sentences with the same subjects.

Bad advice.

Your prose will become monotonous for reasons more serious than repeated Topics or subjects. It will be monotonous if you write one short sentence after another, or one long sentence after another. Your prose will be monotonous if you stuff it with nominalizations and passives. You avoid monotony by saying what you have to say as clearly as you can.

At the risk of asking a question that might invite the wrong answer, did the revised paragraph about Topics, the one with the consistent Topics, seem more monotonous than the original (p. 42)? It has only two main Topics: *Topics* and *reader.* If, as you read that paragraph, your eyes did not glaze over (as a result of the prose style, at any rate), then we have settled the issue of monotony and consistent subjects.

If you attend to this principle of consistently ordering old information before new, you will avoid another problem—subjects that are long and complex because they present new information. Look again at the string of Topics in the pair of paragraphs about Topics. In the original, the subject/Topics are long and complex, partly because they express newer ideas. In the revised version, the subject/Topics are short and specific. Because the Topics in the revised version express familiar information, we could phrase them in a few words, even a single pronoun. If in the Topics of your sentences you refer to ideas that you have already mentioned, your subjects will be consistently short and precise, close to your verbs. And that will get your sentences off to a quick start.

MANAGING SUBJECTS

English provides us with several ways to shorten a long subject, usually by switching it with another, shorter part of the sentence, a part that probably contains information repeated from or referring to a previous sentence. In each of the following pairs of sentences, we revise the first by moving to the end a long subject that expresses important, usually new information. The shorter segment, which we move to the beginning, usually expresses older information, information that typically connects the reader to something that has gone before.

1. Passives again. One important use of the passive is that it lets us replace a long subject full of new information with a short one that repeats something already mentioned or more familiar:

    During the first years of our Republic, *a series of brilliant and virtuous presidents committed to a democracy yet confident of their own special competence* conducted **its administration.**

    During the first years of our Republic, **its administration** was conducted *by a series of brilliant and virtuous presidents committed to a democracy yet confident of their own special competence.*

    Astronomers, physicists, and a host of other researchers entirely familiar with the problems raised by quasars have confirmed **these observations.**

    These observations have been confirmed by *astronomers, physicists, and a host of other researchers entirely familiar with the problems raised by quasars.*

These sentences illustrate the main use of the passive—to improve cohesion and emphasis. Textbooks regularly tell us to avoid passives on general principle. That's more bad advice.

2. Subject-complement switching. Sometimes, we simply switch the subject and complement, especially when what follows the linking verb *be* refers to something already mentioned:

> *The source of the American attitude toward rural dialects* is **more interesting** [than something already mentioned].

> **More interesting** [than something already mentioned] is *the source of the American attitude toward rural dialects*.

We can make a similar switch with a few other verbs:

> The failure of the administration to halt the rising costs of hospital care *lies* **at the heart of the problem.**

> **At the heart of the problem** *lies* the failure of the administration to halt the rising costs of hospital care.

> Some complex issues *run* **through these questions.**

> **Through these questions** *run* some complex issues.

Here are the two principles that are more important than always getting Agents into the subjects of your sentences:

1. Put in the subject/Topic of your sentences ideas that you have already mentioned, or ideas that are so familiar to your readers that if you state them at the beginning of a sentence, you will not surprise them.
2. Keep your Topics consistent. They don't have to be identical. But they should constitute a consistent string of Topics.

Here are two consequences of following these principles:

1. You may find yourself writing as many passive sentences as active. But if the result of having all active sentences is a less consistent sequence of Topics, leave the sentences passive.
2. As noted earlier, you may find yourself using nominalizations as Topics because those nominalizations refer to ideas in sentences that went before. That is an important use of nominalizations: to sum up in one phrase actions you have just mentioned so that you can comment on them. Here's an example:

To account for the relationships among colonies of related samples, it is necessary to track their genetic history through hundreds of generations. *This kind of study* requires that we keep careful histories of all members in the field.

Here is a quick and dirty way to determine how well you have managed your Topics. Run a line under the first five or six words of every sentence (in fact under the subject of every verb in every clause, if you can do it). Read the noun phrases underlined. If any of them seem not to belong to the general set of Topics, then check whether they refer to ideas mentioned toward the end of the previous sentence. If any of the topics seem to jump out as new and unanticipated, consider revising those sentences.

The best diagnosis, however, is your own sensibilities. Prose stuffed with nominalizations and passives has a certain bloated quality. Prose that jumps from Topic to Topic with no plan feels different—disjointed, out of focus. If you are sensitive to how you feel about what you're reading you will develop an instinct for where to look when you feel uneasy about the quality of your writing. Then you will also know where to begin revising.

Exercise 3-1

Revise these passages so that each has a consistent string of Topics. One way to start is to determine first who the major characters are, then locate their significant actions. At that point, you have only to start each sentence with the name of the principal character, and let the sentence take you where it takes you.

1. The crucial importance of language skills in children's problem solving ability was stressed by Jones (1985) in his classic paper on children's thinking. Improvement in non-verbal problem solving occurred as a result of improvements in language skills. It was suggested in that paper that use of previously acquired language habits for problem articulation and activation of knowledge previously learned through language was the source of better performance. Therefore, systematic practice in the verbal formulation of non-linguistic problems prior to attempts at their solution might be an avenue for exploration in the enhancement of problem solving in general.

2. The power to create and communicate a new message to fit a new experience is not part of the power of animals in their natural states. Their genetic code imposes on them only what they can communicate. Information in regard to distance, direction, source richness, in regard to pollen, constitutes the total information content which can be communicated by bees. The same limited repertoire of messages delivered over and over in the same way, for generation after generation, is characteristic of animals of the same species, in all significant respects, in fact.

3. Vegetation covers the earth, except for those areas continuously covered with ice or utterly scorched by continual heat. Richly fertilized plains and river valleys are places where plants grow, as well as at the edge of perpetual snow in high mountains. There is plant growth not only in and around lakes and swamps but under the ocean and next to it. The cracks of busy city sidewalks have plants in them as well as in barren rocks. Before man existed the earth was covered with vegetation, and the earth will have vegetation long after evolutionary history swallows us up.

4. There is a growing resistance to allowing the construction of new mental health outpatient facilities in residential areas. Concern about declines in property values and the loss of tax base property are mentioned most frequently, but a distrust, founded on the notion that the few notorious examples of supervisory failures represent the rule rather than the exception, complicates this problem even further. An extensive campaign to change these perceptions is necessary at this point, in our opinion. At the moment, a figure of approximately $1 m. is our best estimate for the cost of such a campaign.

5. It appears to be the case that current educational practice reflects behavior theory in two ways: First its reflection in official edicts that require learning goals to be stipulated in terms of behavioral objectives, or in terms of the observable behavior that will count as an indication that a student has achieved the desired learning; and second in its use as a method for bringing about learning (behavior modification), a use that stresses appropriate reinforcement schedules, can be commonly found in the literature. The conclusion that we draw in regard to these observations is that one might argue that the assumption behind both of these expressions is that causal terms may describe human action, that thought and feelings, which we so often conceive of as private, are basically public and observable, and that manipulating the causal factors involved can alter behavior.

Now that you understand how important subject/Topics are, you can see why you have to signal them clearly and distinctly. At the beginning of your sentences, you have to subordinate everything else to making clear a consistent, logical string of Topics.

TRANSITIONS/ORIENTERS/LOCATORS

There's no consensus among editors and writers on how best to use transitional words like *therefore, however, nevertheless,* and *but, yet, so.* Some editors suggest that we use many of them; others, few. Some competent writers use them often, others rarely. The more careful we are to organize the sequence of our ideas, the fewer of them we need. But however often you use them, keep them short, use them precisely, and keep them close to the beginning of their sentences, among the first six words. Here are some common transitions:

— Adding: *furthermore, moreover, similarly, and, also.*
— Opposing: *but, however, though, nevertheless, on the other hand*
— Concluding: *so, therefore, for, as a result, consequently*
— Exemplifying: *for example, for instance, to illustrate.*
— Intensifying: *in fact, indeed, even, as a matter of fact.*
— Sequencing: *first, second, finally, in conclusion, to sum up.*

Adding: If you begin a sentence or a paragraph with *also, and,* or *another,* look again. It's not incorrect to start a sentence with **and,** but such a general connector suggests that you may not have thought through how logically you are connecting your ideas; you may be just adding one thought to another. An *also* at the beginning of a sentence can make a sentence seem especially tacked-on:

> Metaphor is one of the most difficult figures of speech for an inexperienced writer to master. *Also,* irony can be a problem.

Be sure your *also* introduces a second item parallel to the preceding one, not an elaboration of the first:

> Metaphor is one of the most difficult figures of speech for an inexperienced writer to master. Also, it requires a mature imagination and a sense of appropriateness.

That *also* doesn't introduce an idea that parallels metaphor, but an idea that elaborates on it. *Because* would be more precise:

. . . an inexperienced writer to master, *because* it requires a mature imagination and a sense of appropriateness.

And avoid beginning more than a few sentences with *and:* Reserve it for places where you want special emphasis, usually at the end of a sequence of points. It can signal your reader that you have come to the last item in a series.

Opposing: Whenever you contradict or qualify a statement, you must signal that qualification early on with *but, however, on the other hand.* A sequence of *buts* can be both awkward and confusing.

> The competition to discover the particular shape of the DNA chain came down to what looked like a dead heat between Linus Pauling and the Watson-Crick team, *but* it was the latter who had the decided advantage of far superior X-ray photographs. *But* even if Pauling had had the same pictures, he probably wouldn't have been able to look at them objectively so committed was he to the concept of a triple helix.

You can avoid a second *but* with a *however,* preferably placed inside the sentence:

> The competition to discover the particular shape of the DNA chain came down to what looked like a dead heat between Linus Pauling and the Watson-Crick team, but it was the latter who had the decided advantage of far superior X-ray photographs. Even if Pauling had the same pictures, however, he probably wouldn't have been able to. . . .

You might also change the second *but* to a *though* and move it a few words into its sentence:

> The competition to discover the particular shape of the DNA chain came down to what looked like a dead heat between Linus Pauling and the Watson-Crick team, but it was the latter who had the decided advantage of far superior X-ray photographs. Even if Pauling had had the same pictures, *though,* he probably wouldn't have been able. . . .

Some writers ask whether they should begin a sentence with *however.* If you do, you do not violate any rule, but the small hesitation that follows *however* will retard a sentence just when you may want it to be accelerating.

Connectors: Use logical connectors such as *therefore, hence, thus* and *then* sparingly. Your ideas should flow clearly enough not to need them, except for special emphasis. Because they are so varied, it might be useful to review their precise meanings:

— *As a result:* The final consequence
— *Consequently:* A peripheral or direct causal result but not necessarily the final one.
— *Therefore:* Signals a step in a logical chain, not in a causal one.
— *Thus, hence, then:* Close to *therefore*
— *So:* Less formal, more general than the others, so it can replace most of them in a casual style.

> The appreciation of the Deutschmark against the dollar has made German imports increasingly expensive. *As a result,* products ranging from Rhine wine to BMWs are no longer selling among the Yuppy set as well as they once did.

> New right-to-privacy laws have made it impossible to compile health data in the ways we have been doing it. *Consequently,* we are no longer able to analyze the real needs of our students.

> You failed to indicate the financial resources of your family. We *therefore* conclude that either you are self-supporting or that you are not requesting scholarship aid.

We can be less formal in any of these sentences with *so,* but we would not use *therefore* in the first and second, or *as a result* in the third.

Orienters: Orienters help a reader by establishing a point of view. We use them to suggest how certain we are:

> *Under certain circumstances,* it is possible to control one's autonomic nervous system.

> *Up to a point,* we are all willing to follow orders.

We use orienters to set the context in which our readers should interpret our claims:

> *From a political point of view,* the President's efforts to bring peace to the Middle East were at best a risky undertaking.

> *Pragmatically,* we would do better to make the package smaller and the price higher.

Locators place the reader in time or place:

> *During the next few years,* America must solve its balance of payments problem.

> *In many parts of the globe,* life is as short and brutal as it was during prehistoric times.

Because all words that orient, locate, and provide transition create context, they are most helpful early in a sentence. At the end of a sentence, they force a reader to create that context retrospectively.

SOME SPECIAL PROBLEMS WITH TOPICS 1:
AUDIENCE AS TOPIC

Occasionally we may have to write for an audience able to understand only the clearest and simplest prose. Or, more often, we have to write on a matter so complex that even a competent reader might find it difficult. To either case, everything we have said applies—an agent/action style, consistent Topics, a predictable flow of old-new information. But we can make our prose more immediate—closer to the reader—if in those sentences we can also make the reader their Topics.

When we write for readers who do not read easily, we are often giving them practical advice—how to do something, such as operate a machine, file a form, or rent a house. Or we may be trying to inform them about significant facts that affect their jobs, employment, politics, or health. Such readers will find information that seems dissociated from their immediate experience too abstract to be meaningful, too distant to be relevant. We can make it immediately relevant for them by bringing those readers into the flow of the discourse, by making *them* agents and goals and *their* experiences the action. Here is some advice on consumerism that appeared in a publication directed to a very broad audience:

> The following information should be verified in every lease before signing: a full description of the premises to be rented and its exact location; the amount, frequency, and dates of payments; the amounts of deposits and pre-payment of rents; a statement setting forth the conditions under which the deposit will be refunded.

That's not particularly difficult for an educated adult. But we can make it clearer—more reader-friendly, if you will—if we bring the reader into the flow of information in the form of *you* (which I have italicized only to highlight it):

When *you* get the lease from the landlord, *you* should not sign it right away. Before *you* sign, do these things:

1. Make sure the lease describes the place that *you* are renting.
2. Make sure the lease tells *you* exactly where the place is.
3. Make sure that the lease tells *you*
   — how much rent *you* have to pay.
   — how often *you* have to pay it.
   — on what day *you* have to pay it.
4. Be sure that the lease tells *you*
   — how much deposit *you* have to give to the landlord before *you* move in.
   — how much rent *you* have to pay before *you* move in.
5. Be sure that the lease tells *you* when the landlord can keep *your* deposit and not give it back to *you*.

I did more than shorten sentences, use simple words, and put agents into subjects, and actions into verbs. I also made the reader and the reader's experience a direct part of the discourse. (I also used a tabular order with lots of white space. Had it been longer, I could have broken it up with headings and subheadings.)

True, though our revision is more readable, it's also longer. But we ought not assume that it's less economical—at least not if we judge economy by a measure more sophisticated than counting words. The real measure of economy should be whether we have achieved our ends, whether our readers understand what we want them to understand or do what we want them to do.

Here is another example that might make the point more convincingly. It's from an actual set of regulations intended to tell train crews how to keep one train from running into another:

When a train is moving on a main track at less than one-half the maximum authorized timetable speed for any train at that location, under circumstances in which it may be overtaken, a crew member must put off single burning fusees at rear of train at intervals that do not exceed the burning time of the fusee. When a train is moving on a main track at or more than one-half the maximum authorized timetable speed for any train at that location, under circumstances in which it may be overtaken, crew members responsible for providing protection must consider grade, track curvature, weather conditions, and speed of the train relative to following trains, when deciding if burning fusees should be put off.

Those two sentences have only three passives and five harmless nominalizations. But those sentences are too long and too packed with information to be clear to a trainman who may never have gone beyond the ninth grade. Indeed, they are a bit much for any reader. This would be clearer (I've again used italics only to highlight the *you's*):

> If (1) *you* are responsible for *your* train, and
> (2) *you* think another train might overtake *you, you* must put off burning fusees from the rear of *your* train.

Follow these guidelines:

Condition.   *You* are on a main track and *you* are moving at **less** than half the speed that the timetable allows for any train at that location.
            Put off single burning fusees often enough so that the second is in place before the first one burns out, and so on.

Condition.   *You* are on a main track, and *you* are moving at **more** than half the speed that the timetable allows at that location.
            Consider these conditions when *you* decide whether you should put off fusees.
            —grade
            —track curvature
            —weather conditions
            —speed of *your* train compared to the speed of a following train

I've broken two long sentences into shorter ones. I've used more space. I've also used a few more words—sixteen. Does that make this version less economical? Not if we balance the cost of the paper against the cost of a couple of trains. Short-term savings don't always mean long-run economy.

Exercise 3–2

1.   In 1985, the Government Accounting Office sponsored a study that inquired into why fewer than half the automobile owners comply with letters that recall their automobiles. That study found that one reason was that car owners could not understand the letters. I received the following automobile recall letter. Revise it to make *you* or *we* the subject of as many verbs as you can.

A defect which involves the possible failure of a frame support plate may exist on your vehicle. This plate (front suspension pivot bar support plate) connects a portion of the front suspension to the vehicle frame, and its failure could affect vehicle directional control, particularly during heavy brake application. In addition, your vehicle may require adjustment service to the hood secondary latch system. The secondary latch may be misaligned so that the hood may not be adequately restrained to prevent hood fly-up in the event the primary latch is inadvertently left unengaged. Sudden hood fly-up beyond the secondary latch while driving could impair driver visibility. In certain circumstances, occurrence of either of the above conditions could result in vehicle crash without prior warning.

2.   Do the same with this next passage. I have boldfaced some significant actions in the first part of this passage. You'll have to pick out the relevant actions in the rest. Note that a good many actions are implied in adjectives: *distributions are fully taxable as ordinary income* means *You will have to pay taxes on the distributions.*

As mentioned earlier, there is an opportunity for a **rollover** of all or part of the lump sum distribution into an IRA and for the **deferral** of **taxation** until distributions are periodically received from the IRA. Note that the **earnings** on the account rolled over will also continue their **growth** on a tax-deferred basis until distribution begins. However, because all distributions from an IRA are fully taxable as ordinary income, **rollovers** into IRAs will generally eliminate any **qualification** for ten-year **averaging** on subsequent distributions. To maximize after-tax retirement cash flow, the choice between a taxfree rollover into an IRA or ten-year forward averaging depends on whether the benefits of tax deferral will be in excess of the benefits of paying a small tax at the time of distribution. The optimal decision can only be made by analyzing several interrelated factors.

SOME SPECIAL PROBLEMS WITH TOPICS 2: DESIGNING TOPICS

It's possible to create subtle effects if you find verbs that let you shift into your subject/Topic position just those words that let you control your audience's point of view. Children learn how quickly:

Tom got in my way, we bumped, my glass dropped, and the milk spilled.

which is to say,

> When I bumped into Tom I dropped my glass and spilled the milk.

Neither sentence is more or less "true" to the facts. Yet while both seem to have an agent-action style, the second assigns responsibility in a way different from the first.

We best appreciate language when we appreciate how skilled writers draw on its resources to achieve subtle ends. Here are the first few sentences of Lincoln's "Gettysburg Address," rewritten from a plausible and coherent but different Topical point of view:

> Four score and seven years ago, *this continent* witnessed the birth of a new nation, conceived in liberty and dedicated to our fathers' proposition that all men are created equal. Now, a *great Civil War* engages us, testing whether *that nation or any nation* so conceived and so dedicated, can long endure. *That War* has provided us with a great battlefield for a meeting place here. *A portion of this field* is to receive its dedication as the final resting place for those who here gave their lives that this nation might live. *This* is altogether a fitting and proper thing to do. But in a larger sense, *this ground* will not let us dedicate, consecrate, or hallow it. *It* has already received that consecration from the brave men, living and dead, who struggled here, far above our poor power to add or detract. *What is said here* will be little noted nor long remembered, but *what those men did here* can never be forgotten.

Compare with the original:

> Four score and seven years ago *our fathers* brought forth on this continent a new nation, conceived in liberty, and dedicated to the proposition that all men are created equal.
>
> Now *we* are engaged in a great civil war, testing whether *that nation,* or any nation so conceived and so dedicated, can long endure. *We* are met on a great battlefield of that war. *We* have come to dedicate a portion of that field as a final resting place for *those who* here gave their lives that *that nation* might live. It is altogether fitting and proper that *we* should do this.
>
> But, in a larger sense, *we* cannot dedicate—*we* cannot consecrate—*we* cannot hallow this ground. *The brave men,* living and dead, who struggled here have consecrated it, far above our poor power to add or detract. *The world* will little note, nor long remember what *we* say here, but *it* can never forget what *they* did here. It is for *us the living,* rather, to be dedicated here to the unfinished work which *they who* fought here have thus far so nobly advanced. It is rather for *us* to be here dedicated to

the great task remaining before us —that from these honored dead *we* take increased devotion to that cause for which *they* gave the last full measure of devotion—that *we* here highly resolve that *these dead* shall not have died in vain—that *this nation,* under God, shall have a new birth of freedom—and that *government of the people, by the people, and for the people,* shall not perish from the earth.

Topics	Predicate
our fathers	brought forth
we	are engaged
that nation	can long endure
we	are met
we	have come
those who	here gave
that nation	might live
we	do this
we	cannot dedicate
we	cannot consecrate
we	cannot hallow
the brave men	have consecrated it
the world	will little note
it (the world)	can never forget
they	did

The Topics of the revision are quite different, but still consistent: they are the locations of the actions or the actions themselves, metaphorically transformed into seeming agents.

this continent	witnessed
a great Civil War	engages us
That War	has provided us
that nation	can endure
a portion of this field	is to receive
this	is altogether a fitting
this ground	will not let us
It	has received
what is said here	will be little noted
what those men did here	can never be forgotten

What's the difference? Lincoln assigned responsibility to his audience. By consistently using *we* to make his audience the agents of the actions, Lincoln topically grouped them with the founding fathers and with the men who fought and died at Gettysburg. By so doing, he tacitly invited his listeners to join their forefathers and their dead countrymen in making the great sacrifices the living must still make if they are to preserve the Union.

My revision shifts agency away from people and assigns it to abstractions and places: **the continent witnesses, a great civil war engages, the war provides, a portion of the field receives.** I have retold Lincoln's story from a different but still coherent point of view, metaphorically investing agency and responsibility in abstract entities. Had Lincoln presented my version, he would have relieved his audience of its profound responsibility to act, and would thereby have deprived us of the greatest speech in our history.

You may think at this point that I am saying we should always design our prose so that Agents act on their own responsibility, that when we deflect responsibility away from people, when we topicalize abstractions, we create prose that is less honest, less direct than prose whose agents act as subject/Topic. If in 1775 Thomas Jefferson had followed that advice, he would have written a very different **Declaration of Independence.** Note in the original how Jefferson has *designed* most of the sentences so that they do not open with the colonists asserting their own actions. Instead, he uses the subject/Topic to refer to events, rights, duties, needs, etc., concepts that make them seem to act as agents serving higher forces:

> When in the Course of human events, it becomes necessary for one people to dissolve the political bands which have connected them with another, and to assume among the powers of the earth, the separate and equal station to which the Laws of Nature and of Nature's God entitle them, a decent respect to the opinions of mankind requires that they should declare the causes which impel them to the separation. We hold these truths to be self-evident, that all men are created equal, that they are endowed by their Creator with certain unalienable Rights, that among these are Life, Liberty and the pursuit of happiness. That to secure these rights, Governments are instituted among Men, deriving their just powers from the consent of the governed, that whenever any Form of government becomes destructive of these ends, it is the Right of the People to alter or to abolish it, and to institute new Government, laying its foundation on such principles and organizing its powers in such form, as to them shall seem most likely to effect their Safety and Happiness. Prudence, indeed, will dictate that Governments long established should not be changed for light and transient causes. . . .

Contrast that with a version in which the colonists are the consistent and independently acting agents/Topic of every action.

> When we decided to dissolve the political bands which connected us with Britain, and to assume among the powers of the earth the separate and equal station which we claim title to through the Laws of Nature and of Nature's God, then if we decently respect the opinions of mankind, we should declare why we have done so. We recognize as self-evident these truths—we are all equal in our creation, that we have from God certain unalienable Rights, and that among these are Life, Liberty and the right to try to be happy. [Try revising the rest of the passage along the same lines.]

In my version, the colonists are acting not because higher principles have forced them to act, but merely because they have decided to. That difference defined a new way of conducting political life in this world, a political life independent of a king, but still dependent on higher powers of Nature and God. The lesson to be drawn here (both politically and stylistically, perhaps) is that all local principles must yield to higher principles. The real problem is recognizing those occasions when we should subordinate one principle to another. That's not something I can help you with. That knowledge comes only with experience.

Exercise 3-3

1. At the beginning of this passage from his essay, "Stranger in the Village," James Baldwin makes the cathedral at Chartres the Topic and metaphorical agency. But then he makes the villagers and himself Topics. Revise so that in the first sentence the villagers and Baldwin are the Topics/subjects/agents. What difference does it make? What other changes of this kind—shifting senses of agency and Topic—are possible? What are the consequences?

   > The cathedral at Chartres, I have said, says something to the people of this village which it cannot say to me, but it is important to understand that this cathedral says something to me which it cannot say to them. Perhaps they are struck by the power of the spires, the glory of the windows; but they have known God, after all, longer than I have known him, and in a different way, and I am terrified by the slippery bottomless well to be found in the crypt,

down which heretics were hurled to death, and by the obscene, inescapable gargoyles jutting out of the stone and seeming to say that God and the devil can never be divorced. I doubt that the villagers think of the devil when they face a cathedral because they have never been identified with the devil. But I must accept the status which myth, if nothing else, gives me in the West before I can hope to change the myth.

2. Revise this passage by the American historian, Frederick Turner, so that the Topics of the sentences constitute a different but still consistent set of Topics/agents/subjects. For example, the first sentence could read,

> The colonist must submit to the wilderness.

Why is it appropriate that at the beginning of the passage, Turner made the wilderness the seeming agency, but that toward the end, he assigned agency to the colonists?

> The wilderness masters the colonist. It finds him a European in dress, industries, tools, modes of travel and thought. It takes him from the railroad car and puts him in the birch canoe. It strips off the garments of civilization and arrays him in the hunting shirt and the moccasin. It puts him in the log cabin of the Cherokee and the Iroquois and runs an Indian palisade around him. Before long, he has gone to planting Indian corn and ploughing with a sharp stick: he shouts the war-cry and takes the scalp in orthodox Indian fashion. In short, the frontier is at first too strong for the man. He must accept the conditions which it furnishes, or perish, and so he fits himself into the Indian clearings and follows the Indian trails. Little by little he overcomes the wilderness, but the outcome is not the old Europe. The fact is, that here is a new product that is American.

3. In this passage, Smith is the consistent subject/agent/Topic. The passage begins,

> On June 30, 1986, William Smith joined Owens Accounting, as a temporary Auditor. At that time, Smith understood from George Owens that. . . .

If we want to focus our reader's attention not on Smith but on Owens, if we want to make Owens the one who consistently acts and thereby is responsible for the situation described, then we can revise this passage in ways that will keep the same plot, but tell a very different story. For example, we could begin our new story like this:

> On June 30, 1986, Owens Accounting hired William Smith as a temporary Auditor. At that time, George Owens explained to Smith. . . .

Revise the rest of this passage to make Owens the consistent agent. In simple terms, revise the passage so that Owens is the acting subject of every sentence. Do not use passive verbs to get Owens into the subject. And do not add or subtract any facts.

> On June 30, 1986, William Smith joined George Owens' company, Owens Accounting, as a temporary Auditor. At that time, Smith understood from George Owens that he (Smith) would advance to permanent Auditor within six months if, in the judgment of Owens, he was performing at a level of competence expected of other Auditors. In this position, Smith worked under the direct supervision of Owens. During this period, he was the subject of careful observations by Owens. Smith, in the opinion of Owens, did not appear to progress as rapidly as appropriate. Smith did not meet with Owens to find out about Owens' evaluations. On January 3, 1987, Smith met with Owens and learned from him that he would not advance to permanent Auditor for at least three months, or until he satisfied Owens that he could perform his job competently. Smith received advice from Owens that he (Smith) could call on Owens for assistance in mastering the job, if Smith desired. Smith claims that he was unreasonably surprised when he received the news that he had been accumulating negative observations that would delay his promotion. Smith had no reason to believe that he was failing to satisfy Owens with his performance and he had had no occasion to learn that fact. He now seeks arbitration under the policy of the firm.

SUMMING UP

1. Generally, use the beginning of your sentences to refer to what you have already mentioned or to knowledge that you can assume you and your reader readily share. Compare these:

The huge number of wounded and dead in *the Civil War* exceeded

all the *other wars in American history*. One of the reasons for the
lingering animosity between North and South today is *the memory
of this terrible carnarge.*

Of *all the wars in American history,* none has exceeded *the Civil
War* in the huge number of wounded and dead. *The memory of
this terrible carnage* is one of the reasons for the animosity
between North and South today.

2.   Put transitional words such as *therefore, on the other hand, of
course,* close to the beginning of your sentences.

The memory of this terrible carnage is one of the reasons for the
animosity between North and South today. This century old hostility is manifested in ways that are often indirect, and therefore often
misunderstood, *however.*

The memory of this terrible carnage is one of the reasons for the
animosity between North and South today. *However,* this century-
old hostility is manifested in ways that are often indirect and therefore, often misunderstood.

3.   Put orienting words and phrases such as *for the most part, in the
early part of the Christian era, economically speaking,* at the beginning of your sentences. Keep them short.

We may project particular latent attitudes that we have been taught
onto traits of culture and personality that we believe characterize
the other, *depending on our background.*

Depending on our background, we may project particular latent
attitudes we have been taught onto traits of culture and personality
that we believe characterize the other.

4.   Choose Topics that will control your reader's point of view. How
well you do this will depend on how creatively you can use verbs to
make one or another of your characters the seeming agent of an
action. Which of these would better serve the needs of a patient suing
a physician is obvious:

A patient whose reactions go unmonitored may also claim physician liability. In this case, a patient took Cloromax as prescribed,
which resulted in partial renal failure. The manufacturer's literature indicated that the patient should be observed frequently and

should immediately report any sign of infection. Evidence indicated that the patient had not received instructions to report any signs of urinary blockage. Moreover, the patient had no white cell count taken until after he developed the blockage.

If a physician does not monitor his patient's reactions, he may be held liable. In this case, the physician prescribed Cloromax, which caused the patient to experience partial renal failure. The physician had been cautioned by the manufacturer's literature that he should observe the patient frequently and instruct the patient to report any sign of infection. Evidence indicates that the physician also did not instruct the patient to report any sign of urinary blockage. Moreover, he took no white cell count until after the patient developed the blockage.

The general guiding principle—not the binding rule—is this:

Topic		
Old		New
Subject	Verb	Complement
Cast of characters	Action	

Keep in mind that these are not rules that bind, but principles that guide.

The Grammar
of Emphasis

All's well that ends well.
WILLIAM SHAKESPEARE

In the end is my beginning.
T. S. ELIOT

ACHIEVING EMPHASIS AND STRENGTH

If you begin a sentence well, the end will almost take care of itself. So the first step toward a style that is clear, direct, and coherent lies in how you manage the first few words of every sentence. If at the beginning of your sentences, you consistently organize your subject/Topics around a few central characters or concepts and then move quickly to close that subject with a precise verb expressing a crucial action, then by default you will have to put important new information at the **ends** of your sentences. If you do not manage the flow of your ideas in this way, your prose will seem not just unfocused, but weak, anticlimactic. Compare these two sentences:

> A charge of gross violation of academic responsibility is required for a Board of Trustees to dismiss a tenured faculty member for cause, and an elaborate hearing procedure with a prior statement of charges is provided for before a tenured faculty member may be dismissed for cause, in most States.

> In most States, before a Board of Trustees may dismiss a tenured faculty member for cause, it must charge him with a gross violation of academic responsibility and provide him with a statement of charges and an elaborate hearing procedure.

The first trails off; the second builds a climactic rhythm.

Because the elements that open a sentence serve so many roles, we named them: *orienter, locator,* and most importantly, *Topic.* Since the end of a sentence plays a role no less crucial, we should give it a name as well. When you utter a sentence, your voice naturally rises and falls. When you approach a break in the flow of words, particularly near the end, you ordinarily raise your pitch on one of those last few words and stress it a bit more strongly than you do the others:

                                                    o
. . . a bit more strongly than the
                                                            thers.

This rising pitch and stress signal the end of a sentence. We'll call that part of a sentence plays a role no less crucial, we should give it a name as well. segment its Stress.

MANAGING ENDINGS

We manage the information in this stressed part of the sentence in several ways. We can put our most important information there in the first place. More often, we have to revise our sentences to give the right information the right emphasis.

1. **Trim the end.**
    In some cases, we can just lop off final unnecessary words until we get to the information we want to stress, leaving that information in the final stressed position.

> Sociobiologists are making the provocative claim that our genes largely determine our social behavior in the way we act in situations we find around us every day.

Since *social behavior* means the way we act, we can just drop everything after *behavior:*

> Sociobiologists are making the provocative claim that our genes largely determine our social behavior.

2. **Shift less important information to the left.**
    One way to revise for emphasis is to move unimportant phrases away from the end of a sentence to expose what you want to emphasize:

> The data that are offered to establish the existence of ESP do not make believers of us *for the most part.*

> *For the most part,* the data that are offered to establish the existence of ESP do not make us believers.

Occasionally, we may have to separate subjects from verbs or verbs from objects. This sentence ends weakly:

> No one can explain why that first primeval superatom exploded and thereby created the universe in a few words.

The modifier of *explain, in a few words,* is much shorter than the object of *explain,* the clause *why that first primeval superatom exploded and there-*

by created the universe. To create a smoother flow, we put that short, less important modifier before the longer, more important object, even if we have to split the object from its verb:

> No one can explain *in a few words* why that first primeval superatom exploded and thereby created the universe.

3.   **Shift important information to the right.**

Moving the important information to the end of the sentence is another way to manage the flow of ideas. And the sentence you just read illustrates a missed opportunity. This is more cohesive and emphatic:

> Another way you can manage the flow of ideas is to move the most important information to the end of the sentence.

In fact, this is just the other side of something we've already seen— how to move old information to the beginning of a sentence. Sentences that introduce a paragraph or a new section are frequently of an X *is* Y form. One part, usually older information, glances back at what has gone before; the other announces something new. As we have seen, the older information should come first, the newer last. When it doesn't, we can often reverse the order of subjects and what follows the verb:

> Those questions relating to the ideal system for providing instruction in home computers **are** just as confused.

> Just as confused **are** those questions relating to the ideal system for providing instruction in home computers.

The switch not only puts the reference to the preceding sentences, *Just as confused* early, but it also puts at the end information that the next several sentences will probably address.

> . . . instruction in home computers. For example, should the instruction be connected to some source of information, or. . . .

Some subjects contain a relative clause full of important information that you can shift to the end:

> A discovery *that will change the course of world history and the very foundations of our understanding of ourselves and our place in the scheme of things* is imminent.

> A discovery is imminent *that will change the course of world history and the very foundations of our understanding of ourselves and our place in the scheme of things.*

Don't shift the clause if it creates an ambiguous construction. In this sentence, the italicized clause seems to modify *staff:*

> A marketing approach has been developed by the staff *that will provide us with a new way of looking at our current problems.*

4.   Extract and isolate.

When you put your most important ideas in the middle of a long sentence, the sentence will swallow them up. A way to recover the appropriate emphasis is to break the sentence in two, either just before or just after that important idea. Then revise the new sentences so that you guide your reader to the crucial information. That often means you have to isolate the point of a long sentence by putting it into a shorter sentence of its own.

> Under the Clean Water Act, the EPA will promulgate new standards for the treatment of industrial wastewater prior to its discharge into sewers leading to publicly owned treatment plants, with pretreatment standards for types of industrial sources being discretionary, depending on local conditions, instead of imposing nationally uniform standards now required under the Act.

First, break up the sentence:

> Under the Clean Water Act, the EPA will promulgate new standards for the treatment of industrial wastewater prior to its discharge into sewers that lead to publicly owned treatment plants. Standards for types of industrial sources will be discretionary. They will depend on local conditions, instead of imposing the nationally uniform standards now required under the act.

Then rearrange to get the right emphasis:

> Under the Clean Water Act, the EPA will promulgate new standards for the treatment of industrial wastewater before it is discharged into sewers leading to publicly owned treatment plants. Unlike the standards now required under the act, the new standards will not be uniform across the whole nation. They instead will be discretionary, depending on local conditions.

The point here is the discretionary nature of the rules and their dependence on local conditions—two ideas that the next sentences will probably expand on. So we express that point in its own sentence and put it at the end, in the stress position.

When we ignore these principles of old and new information, we risk writing prose that is both confusing and weak. Read these next few sentences aloud. Hear how your voice trails off into a lower note when at the ends of the sentences, you have to repeat words that you read earlier— *infringe on patents,* etc. Then listen to how the rewritten version lifts your voice up and then brings it down emphatically on the words that ought to be stressed.

> In 1972, the United States Supreme Court declared that components of a patented assembly could be produced in this country without infringing on US patents. Since then, several cases have tested whether various combinations of imported and domestic items could be produced without infringing on US patents. The courts have consistently held any combination would infringe on patents. However, the concept of local production and foreign assembly has not been tested as to infringement on patents.

> In 1972, the United States Supreme Court declared that components of a patented assembly could be produced in this country without infringing on US patents. Since then, this concept has been tested by several cases involving various combinations of imported and domestic items. The courts have consistently held that US patents would be infringed by any combination. What has not been tested, however, is the concept of local production and foreign assembly.

Some Syntactic Devices

There are a few grammatical patterns that add weight to the end of a sentence.

1. **There.**

I wrote the sentence above without realizing that I had illustrated this first pattern. I could have written,

> A few grammatical patterns add weight to the end of a sentence.

If you begin too many sentences with "There is" or "There are," your prose will become flat-footed, lacking movement or energy. But you can open a sentence with *there* in order to push to the end of that sentence those ideas that the next sentences will build on. In other words, like the first sentence of this section, a *there-* sentence lets you introduce the topics for the **following** string of sentences. Again, you may remember someone telling you not to begin sentences with *there.* More bad advice. Like passives, *there-* constructions have a function: to stress those ideas that you intend to develop in following sentences.

2.   **What**

A *what-* sentence throws special emphasis on what follows a linking verb. Compare the emphasis of:

> This country needs a monetary policy that will end the violent fluctuations in money supply, unemployment, and inflation.

> What this country needs is a monetary policy that will end the violent fluctuations in money supply, unemployment, and inflation.

You have to pay for this added emphasis with a few more words, so use the pattern sparingly.

3.   *It-* **shift 1.**

By using *it* as a fill-in subject, you can shift a long introductory clause that would otherwise have been the subject to a position after the verb:

> *That domestic oil prices must eventually rise to the level set by OPEC* once seemed inevitable.

> *It* once seemed inevitable *that domestic oil prices must eventually rise to the level set by OPEC.*

4.   *It-* **shift 2.**

With this pattern, you simultaneously select and emphasize a Topic and throw added weight on the Stress. Compare:

> In 1933 this country experienced a depression that almost wrecked our democratic system of government.

> *It* was **in 1933** that this country experienced a depression that almost wrecked our democratic system of government.

> *It was* **this country** that in 1933 experienced a depression that almost wrecked our democratic system of government.

Because all these syntactic patterns are so self-conscious and because a few of them actually obscure Topics, use them sparingly.

When All Else Fails

If you find yourself stuck with a sentence that ends flatly because you have to repeat a phrase you used in a previous sentence, at least try changing the phrase to a pronoun:

> When the rate of inflation dropped in 1983, large numbers of investors fled to the bond market and invested in *stocks*. However, those particularly interested in the high tech market often did not carefully investigate *the stocks*.

> When the rate of inflation dropped in 1983, large numbers of investors fled the bond market and invested in *stocks*. However, those particularly interested in the high tech market often did not carefully investigate *them*.

By substituting the pronoun for the lightly stressed, repeated word, you throw the emphasis on the word before the pronoun.

Finally, avoid ending a sentence with metadiscourse. Nothing ends a sentence more anticlimactically, as we see:

> The opportunities we offer are particularly rich at the graduate level, it must be remembered.

> The opportunities we offer are, it must be remembered, particularly rich at the graduate level.

Exercise 4–1

Revise these sentences so that those concepts that deserve the most emphasis appear at the end. In the first five, I have boldfaced those elements that I think should be stressed. Eliminate any wordiness, unnecessary nominalization, etc.

1. **The judiciary's tendency to rewrite the Constitution** is the most significant danger in the republic, in my opinion, at least.
2. **A wholly new judicial philosophy that could well affect our society into the 21st century** may well emerge from these studies, if they are studied with the seriousness they deserve.
3. There are **limited** opportunities for teachers to work with individual students in large American colleges and universities.
4. As used in the foundry industry, "turnkey" means **responsibility for**

the satisfactory performance of a piece of equipment in addition to the manufacture and installation of that equipment, according to everyone who understands the matter.

5. Several upper and lower eyelid reconstruction evaluation studies are presented with the aforementioned summary discussions for your general information, in addition.

6. Overbuilding of suburban housing developments has led to the existence of extensive and widespread flooding and economic disaster in parts of our country in recent years, it is now clear.

7. The teacher who makes an assignment of a long final term paper at the end of the semester and who then gives only a grade at the end and nothing else such as a critical comment is a common complaint among people who take college courses.

8. Engine fuel lines and steam heating systems in the older-type coaches also have been known to become choked with this kind of ice under these particular conditions.

9. Renting textbooks for basic required courses rather than buying them—such as mathematics, foreign languages, and English—whose textbooks do not experience change from year to year is possible and feasible, however, economically speaking.

10. The outcome of the war was changed as a result of an event that occurred at about this same point in time, on the other hand.

11. The effective disposal of product materials that are not such that they are found to undergo biodegradation in the environmental ecological system is a question of a different nature, we believe.

12. Guidelines set forth in the MLA style sheet and the NCTE guidelines for the nonsexist use of language should be adhered to by speakers and writers, to the best of their ability.

13. With the fastest growing population in the region, DuPage County covers 338 square miles of land area beginning about 16 miles west of the Chicago loop.

14. An attorney who will feel a certain responsiveness to your needs and interests and who has the capability for translating your organizational problems into the most suitable legal form is your first step, according to most lawyers.

Exercise 4-2

Revise these passages so that they end with what you believe deserves most emphasis, as well as begin with appropriate Topics.

1. The story of King Lear and his three daughters was a popular one during the reign of Queen Elizabeth. At least a dozen easily available books offered the story to anyone wishing to read it, by the time Elizabeth died. The characters were undeveloped in most of these stories, however, making the story a simple narrative that explicitly stated obvious morals. When he began work on *Lear,* one of his great tragedies, Shakespeare must have had several versions of this story readily available to him. He turned the characters into credible human beings with complex motives, however, even though they were based on the stock figures of the legend.

2. Whether the date an operation intends to close down might be part of management's duty to disclose during contract bargaining is the issue here, it would appear. The minimization of conflict is the central rationale for the duty that management has to bargain in good faith. In order to allow the union to put forth proposals on behalf of its members, companies are obligated to disclose major changes in an operation during bargaining, though the case law is scanty on this matter.

3. Athens' catastrophic Sicilian Invasion is the most important event in Thucydides' *History of the Peloponnesian War.* Three-quarters of the history is devoted to setting up the invasion of Sicily because of this. Through the step-by-step decline in Athenian society that Thucydides describes we can see in particular how Thucydides chose to anticipate the Sicilian Invasion. What need was there to anticipate the invasion? The inevitability that we associate with the Greek tragic drama is the basic reason.

This next passage may seem difficult, because it probably deals with subject matter distant from what you know. That doesn't matter. Even if you don't fully understand the words, you can still revise it to make it more readable. When you learn the major principles of clear, readable prose, you can apply those principles to prose of any kind.

4. Mucosal and vascular permeability altered by a toxin elaborated by the vibrio is one current hypothesis to explain this kind of severe condition. Changes in small capillaries located near the basal surface of the epithelial cells, and the appearance of numerous micro-vesicles in the cytoplasm of the mucosal cells is evidence in favor of this hypothesis. Hydrodynamic transport of fluid into the interstitial tissue and then through the mucosa into the lumen of the gut is believed to depend on altered capillary permeability.

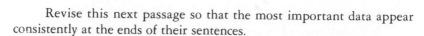
Revise this next passage so that the most important data appear consistently at the ends of their sentences.

5. Changes in revenues are as follows. An increase to $56,792 from $32,934, a net increase of approximately 73%, was realized July 1-August 31 in the Ohio and Kentucky areas. In the Indiana and Illinois areas there was in the same period a 10% increase of $15,370, from $153,281 to $168,651. However, a decrease to $190,580 from $200,102, or 5%, occurred in the Wisconsin and Minnesota regions in almost the same period of time.

CONTROLLING THE NUANCES OF EMPHASIS 1: HARD WORDS

When we write highly technical prose, we often write to an audience that understands as well as we do—or better—the complex terminology, the background, the habits of mind that workers in that field have to control. When we do, we don't have to explain technical terms as we would to a layperson.

But the problem in writing for a non-expert audience is more complex than merely defining strange terms. If for a non-expert audience I used terms like *sarcomere, tropomyosin,* and *myoplasm,* I would not only have to define them; I would also have to take care to locate those words at that point where my reader is most ready to receive them—at the end of a sentence.

In these next two passages, underline each term that you do not understand. Once you have underlined the occurrence of a term, don't underline it again in that passage. (As you read the second passage, assume you are reading it for the first time.) Then generalize: Where in the two passages do the technical terms typically occur? How does that difference affect how easily you can read the two versions? What other devices did I use to revise the first into the second? One sentence in the second still has all the characteristics of prose written for an insider: which one?

An appreciation of the effects of calcium blockers can best be attained by an understanding of the activation of muscle groups. The proteins actin, myosin, tropomyosin, and troponin make up the sarcomere, the fundamental unit of muscle contraction. Its thick filament is composed of myosin, which is an ATPase or energy producing protein. Actin, tropomyosin, and troponin make up the thin filament. There is a close association between the regulatory proteins, tropomyosin and troponin, and the contractile protein, actin, in the thin filament. The interaction of actin and myosin is controlled by tropomyosin. Troponin I, which participates in the interaction between actin and myosin; troponin T, which binds troponin to tropomyosin; and troponin C, which binds calcium, constitute the three peptide chains of troponin. An excess of 10^{-7} for the myoplasmic concentration of Ca^{++} leads to its binding to troponin C. The inhibitory forces of tropomyosin are removed, and the complex interaction of actin and myosin is manifested as contraction.

When your muscles contract, they use calcium. When you understand how calcium helps activate your muscles, you can appreciate how certain drugs block the effect of calcium, drugs that we call calcium blockers.

The fundamental unit of muscle contraction is the sarcomere. The sarcomere has two filaments, one thick and one thin. These filaments are composed of two kinds of proteins. They are proteins that cause a muscle to contract and proteins that prevent a muscle from contracting. The thick filament of the sarcomere contains the contractile protein myosin. It is an energy producing, or ATPase protein. The thin filament contains another contractile protein, actin. A muscle contracts when the contractile protein myosin interacts with contractile protein actin.

The thin filament also contains two proteins that regulate or prevent contraction. They are the regulatory proteins tropomyosin and troponin. Troponin has three peptide chains:

    (1) troponin I, which participates in the interaction between actin and myosin;

    (2) troponin T, which binds troponin to tropomyosin; and

    (3) troponin C, which binds calcium.

When your muscle relaxes, the regulatory protein tropomyosin in the thin filament inhibits the actin in the thin filament from interacting with the myosin in the thick filament.

When the concentration of Ca^{++} in the myoplasm in the sarcomere exceeds 10^{-7}, the calcium binds to troponin C. The tropomyosin then no longer inhibits actin from interacting with myosin, and your muscle contracts.

For the novice in muscle chemistry, the second version is more readable than the first. Yet both have the same technical terms. In fact, the second has no more information than the first. The versions differ, however, in two ways:

    (1) in the second, I made explicit some of the information that the first only implied—the sarcomere has thick and thin fila-

ments—or information that was indirectly stated in an adjective—converting *regulatory protein* into *proteins that regulate.*

(2) In the second, I introduced technical terms **at the ends of their sentences.**

So in addition to everything we learned in Lessons 2 and 3, here is another key to communicating complex information that requires terminology unfamiliar to your readers: When you introduce a technical term for the first time—or even a familiar but very important term, design a sentence so that you can locate that term at the end, in its stress, **never at the beginning, in its Topic,** even if you have to invent a sentence simply for the sake of defining or emphasizing that term.

Writers often introduce terms in this same way even in highly technical writing for a relatively specialized audience. This passage is from an article in *The New England Journal of Medicine* (note as well the metadiscourse *we*):

> We have previously described a method for generating lymphocytes with antitumor reactivity. The incubation of peripheral-blood lymphocytes with a lymphokine, interleukin-2, generates lymphoid cells that can lyse fresh, noncultured, natural-killer-cell-resistant tumor cells but not normal cells. We have termed these cells lymphokine-activated killer (LAK) cells.

Exercise 4–3

Make a passage from a relatively technical article in a field with which you are reasonably familiar accessible to a generally educated reader.

CONTROLLING THE NUANCES OF EMPHASIS 2: RHETORICAL STRESS

Compare these two passages. One of them was written by W. Averell Harriman for an article in the *New York Times,* January 1, 1984.

> The Administration has blurred the issue of verification—so central to arms control. Irresponsible charges, innuendo and leaks have submerged serious problems with Soviet compliance. The objective, instead, should be not to exploit these concerns in order to further poison our relations, repudiate existing agreements, or, worse still, terminate arms control

altogether, but to clarify questionable Soviet behavior and insist on compliance.

The issue of verification—so central to arms control—has been blurred by the Administration. Serious problems with Soviet compliance have been submerged in irresponsible charges, innuendo and leaks. The objective, instead, should be to clarify questionable Soviet behavior and insist on compliance—not to exploit these concerns in order to further poison our relations, repudiate existing agreements, or, worse still, terminate arms control altogether.

In the original article, Harriman was attacking what he believed were the President's misguided policies. Look at the way the sentences in the two versions end, at what each stresses. As you have probably guessed, Harriman's version is the second one, the one that stresses *blurred by the Administration, irresponsible charges, innuendo and leaks, poison our relations . . . terminate arms control altogether.* It is this second version in which Harriman comes down hard not on references to the Soviet Union, but on references to a Republican administration.

Of course, it is precisely this ability to control emphasis that also lets us *soften* impact, to dilute our emphasis. Compare the effect of these two passages:

At the outset, this penalty might not appear to be particularly onerous. However, we are troubled by the "six months in county jail" rather than the $500 fine. The fact that the violations are criminal in nature concerns us, even though no jail sentences have been imposed so far on an Abco officer. It is appropriate that on the basis of these dangers, the way these alleged criminal violations are dealt with be re-evaluated.

At the outset, you might not feel that this penalty is particularly onerous. We are troubled, however, not by the $500 fine but by the "six months in county jail." Even though no Abco executive officer has received a jail sentence so far, we are concerned that the violations are criminal in nature. These dangers make it appropriate that you re-evaluate the way you deal with these alleged criminal violations.

The first version was in fact written by a very junior person in a very large corporation to a very, very senior person, someone who could indeed spend "six months in county jail" but did not much want to hear about it. And so that junior person was understandably uneasy about coming on hard. The second version is more specific, less passive, etc. But just as important, it also extracts the business about jail and criminal violations from inside the sentences and puts it at the end, where the sentences can by their very structure hammer home some nasty truths.

My point here is not that being mealy-mouthed is always bad; sometimes we have to hedge, be indirect, avoid being emphatic. Rather my point is that just as we can achieve fine nuances of Topic and seeming agency by controlling how we begin sentences, so can we achieve fine nuances of emphasis by controlling how we end them. To soften and obscure, we do not name our cast of characters in our Topics, and we tuck into the middle of a sentence all the information that we don't want our readers to dwell on. Look back at the automobile recall letter on p. 55, and underline the words that carry the bad news: *failure, vehicle crash, affect vehicle directional control,* etc. At what point in individual sentences does the frightening information typically occur?

SUMMING UP

1. Cohesion
   a. Within paragraphs, try to make your Topics a coherent sequence of ideas. Don't hesitate to repeat the same subject through a series of consecutive sentences.
   b. Put connecting words such as *therefore, thus, consequently, those, another,* etc. close to the beginning of their sentences.
   c. Most importantly, put at the end of a sentence the information you intend to develop in the next sentence.
2. Emphasis
   a. Put your important ideas at the end of your sentence, and if your sentence has several clauses, arrange the ideas inside each clause so that the most important ones come last.
   b. Don't write all long or all short sentences. If you do, you will provide too few or too many points of emphasis.

THE SYSTEM OF CLARITY

By now, we begin to appreciate the extraordinary complexity of an ordinary English sentence. A sentence is more than its subject, verb, and object. It is more than the sum of its words and parts. It is a system of systems whose parts we can fit together in very delicate ways to achieve very

delicate ends—if we know how. We can match, mismatch, or metaphorically manipulate the grammatical units and their related semantic
meanings:

subject	verb	
cast of characters	action	

We can match or mismatch rhetorical units to create more or less
important meanings:

topic	stress
old/less important	new/more important

And we can fit these two systems into a larger system:

topic		stress	
old/less important		new/more important	
subject	verb		
cast of characters	action		

Of course, we don't want every one of our sentences to march
lockstep across the page in a rigid agency-action/old-new order. When we
exercise our metaphoric imagination in the way we did with the Gettysburg Address and the Baldwin passage, we can create and control fine
shades of emphasis, agency, action, and point of view.

But if for no good reason you write sentences that consistently depart
from that pattern, if you consistently hide agency, nominalize active verbs
into passive nominalizations, if you consistently end sentences on secondary information, you will find yourself writing prose that is not just
confused and unclear, but prose that lacks any sense of cohesion, coherence,
or emphasis.

In fact, when we stand back from the details of subjects, agents,
passives, nominalizations, Topic and Stress, when we **listen** to our prose,
we should hear something beyond sheer clarity and coherence. We should
hear a **voice**. The voice our readers hear contributes substantially to the

character we project—or more accurately, to the character our readers construct out of what they hear.

Some teachers of writing want to make voice a moral choice between a false voice and the voice "authentic." I suspect that we all speak in many voices, no one of which is more or less false, more or less authentic than another. When you want to be pompous and authoritative, then that's in the voice you project because that's who you are being. When you want to be laconic and direct, then you should be able to adopt that voice. The problem is to hear the voice you are projecting and to change it when you want to. That's no more false than choosing how you dress, how you behave, how you live.

The Grammar of Concision

Less is more.
ROBERT BROWNING

There is no artifice as good and desirable as simplicity.
ST. FRANCIS DE SALES

The love of economy is the root of all virtue.
GEORGE BERNARD SHAW

Let thy words be few.
ECCLESIASTES 5:2

Loquacity and lying are cousins.
GERMAN PROVERB

To a Snail: If "compression is the first grace of style," you have it.
MARIANNE MOORE

Once you can use the structure of a sentence to organize your ideas, you're a long way toward a clear and direct style. But some sentences enjoy all the virtues of grammatical clarity yet remain wordy and graceless. Even when you arrange their grammatical bones in all the right ways, they can still succumb to acute prolixity:

> The point I want to make here is that we can see that American policy in regard to foreign countries as the State Department in Washington and the White House have put it together and made it public to the world has given material and moral support to too many foreign factions in other countries that have controlled power and have then had to give up the power to other factions that have defeated them.

That is,

> Our foreign policy has backed too many losers.

In the longer version, the writer matches agents and actions to subjects and verbs. But she uses ten words where one would have served.

To write clearly, we have to know not only how to manage the flow of ideas but also how to express them concisely. These two principles are easier to state than to follow:

1. Usually, compress what you mean into the fewest words.
2. Don't state what your reader can easily infer.

We inflate our prose in so many ways that it's no use trying to list them all. But you might find it helpful to know the most common kinds of wordiness. This sentence illustrates most of them:

> In my personal opinion, we must listen to and think over in a punctilious manner each and every suggestion that is offered to us.

First, an opinion can only be personal, so we can cut *personal*. And since any statement is implicitly opinion, we can cut *in my opinion*. *Basically* means nothing here, so we cut that too. *Listen to and think over* means *consider*, and *in a punctilious manner* means *punctiliously*, which means no more than *carefully*. *Each and every* is a redundant pair; we need only *each*. A *suggestion* is by definition something offered, and offered to someone, so neither do we need *that is offered to us*. What's left is much leaner,

> We must consider each suggestion carefully.

SOME SIMPLE SOURCES OF WORDINESS

In the following cases, you can just cross out useless words. You will have to rewrite little, if at all.

Redundant Pairs

English has a long tradition of doubling words, a habit that we acquired shortly after we began to borrow from Latin and French the thousands of words that we have since incorporated into English. Because the borrowed word usually sounded a bit more learned than the familiar native one, early writers would use both. Among the common pairs are *full and complete, true and accurate, hopes and desires, hope and trust, each and every, first and foremost, any and all, various and sundry, basic and fundamental, questions and problems,* and, *and so on and so forth.*

Redundant Modifiers

Every word implies another. *Finish* implies *complete,* so *completely finish* is redundant. *Memories* imply *past,* so *past memories* is redundant. *Different* implies *various,* so *various different* is redundant. *Each* implies *individual,* so *each individual* is redundant. Other examples are *basic fundamentals, true facts, important essentials, future plans, personal beliefs, consensus of opinion, sudden crisis, terrible tragedy, end result, final outcome, initial preparation, free gift.* In every case, we simply prune the redundant modifier. Compare:

> We should not try to anticipate *in advance* those great events that will *completely* revolutionize our society because *past* history tells us that it has been the *ultimate* outcome of little events that has *unexpectedly* surprised us.
>
> We should not try to anticipate those great events that will revolutionize our society because history tells us that it has been the effect of little events that has most surprised us.

Redundant Categories

Specific words imply their general categories, so we usually don't have to state both. We know that time is a period, that the mucous membrane is an area, that pink is a color, and that shiny is an appearance. So we don't have to write.

> During that *period of time*, the *mucous membrane area* became *pink in color* and *shiny in appearance.*

but only,

> During that *time*, the *mucous membrane* became *pink* and *shiny.*

In some cases, we can eliminate a general category by changing an adjective into an adverb:

> The holes must be aligned in an *accurate manner.*

> The holes must be *accurately* aligned.

And in some cases, we can change an adjective into a noun and drop the redundant noun:

> The *educational process* and *athletic activities* are the responsibility of *county governmental systems.*

> *Education* and *athletics* are the responsibility of *county governments.*

In each case we delete the general noun and leave the more specific word.
　　Here are some general nouns often used redundantly. In every case, we can be more direct and concise by dropping the general word:

> large in **size,** of a bright **color,** heavy in **weight,** round in **shape,** at an early **time.**

> odd in **appearance,** of a cheap **quality,** honest **in character,** of an uncertain **condition,** in a confused **state,** unusual in **nature,** extreme in **degree,** of a strange **type.**

> curative **process,** regulation **system,** economics **field, area** of mathematics, criminal **problem.**

Meaningless Modifiers

Some modifiers are verbal tics that we use almost as unconsciously as we clear our throats—words and phrases such as *kind of, really, basically, definitely, practically, actually, virtually, generally, certain, particular, individual, given, various, different, specific, for all intents and purposes.*

> *For all intents and purposes,* American industrial productivity *generally* depends on *certain* factors that are *really* more psychological *in kind* than of any *given* technological aspect.

When we prune both the empty nouns and meaningless modifiers, we have a clearer and sharper sentence:

> American industrial productivity depends more on psychology than on technology.

Pompous Diction

Replacing unnecessarily formal words with more common ones may not reduce wordiness, but you will make your diction sharper and more direct.

> Pursuant to the recent memorandum issues August 9, 1987, because of financial exigencies, it is incumbent upon us all to endeavor to make maximal utilization of telephonic communication in lieu of personal visitation.

All of that means only,

> As the memo of August 9 said, to save the company money, use the telephone as much as you can instead of making personal visits.

There is a common word for almost every fancy borrowed one. When we pick the ordinary word we rarely lose anything important.

Sometimes, of course, the more obscure, more formal word is exactly the right one:

> We tried to negotiate in good faith but the union remains utterly intransigent.

Intransigent is not synonymous with *stubborn* or *firm* or *fixed* or *unyielding* or *uncompromising.* It means to adopt an *unreasonably* fixed position. We can, for example, be uncompromising about our moral behavior, but we would not want to say that we were *intransigent* about it, for that would suggest that we *should* compromise. So if we mean intransigent, then we should use *intransigent.*

More often, though, we choose the big word not for its precision but for its learned weight. Thus the sportscaster who intones,

> His pugilistic exploits supersede even the zenith attained by that memorable and unforgettable nonpareil of athletic endeavor, Sugar Ray Robinson.

or the police officer who reports,

> The alleged felon effectuated entrance into the domicile by means of an appliance forcibly applied to the external locking mechanism.

In a formal situation, most of us choose excessively formal language to compensate for our linguistic insecurity. We can deplore the choice and urge the writer to find simpler words. But we ought to think twice before we ridicule him. It's a natural impulse that, given the right circumstances, any of us will yield to.

A smattering of big words and their simpler near-synonyms:

Contingent upon—dependent on	Deem—think
Endeavor—try	Envisage—think, regard, see
Utilization—use	Avert to—mention
Termination—end	Apprise—inform
Initiate—begin	Eventuate—happen
Is desirous of—wants	Transpire—happen
Cognizant of—aware of	Render—make, give, give back
Ascertain—find out	
Facilitate—help	Transmit—send
Implement—start, create, carry out, begin	Prior to—before
	Subsequent to—after

Exercise 5-1

Prune the redundancy from these sentences.

1. These various agencies and offices that provide aid and assistance services to persons who participate in our program activities have reversed themselves back from the policy that they recently announced to return to the original policy that they followed earlier.
2. It is necessary that all critics cannot avoid employing complex and abstract terms in order for them to successfully analyze literary texts and discuss them in a basically meaningful way.
3. Scientific endeavor in general depends on true and fully accurate data if it is to offer theories that will allow mankind to advance forward into the future in a safe and cautious way.

4. It is true that in spite of the fact that the educational environment is a very significant and important facet to each and every one of our children in terms of his or her own individual future development and growth, different groups and people do not all support certain tax assessments at a reasonable and fair rate that are required for the purpose of providing an educational context at a decent level of quality.

5. Most likely, a majority of all the patients who appear at the public medical clinic facility do not expect specialized medical attention and treatment because their health problems and concerns often seem not to be of a major nature and can for the most part usually be adequately treated with enough proper understanding and attention.

SOME COMPLEX KINDS OF WORDINESS

In these next cases, you have to think about your prose more carefully and then rewrite more extensively.

Belaboring the Obvious

Often, we are diffusely redundant, needlessly stating what everyone knows.

> Imagine a mental picture of someone engaged in the intellectual activity of trying to learn what the rules are for how to play the game of chess.

Imagine implies a mental picture; *trying to learn* implies being engaged in the activity of; we know chess is intellectual; everyone knows that *chess* is a game and that games are played. The less redundant version:

> Imagine someone trying to learn the rules of chess.

Or consider this:

> When you write down your ideas, keep in mind that the audience that reads what you have to say will infer from your writing style something about your character.

You can write down only ideas; your audience can read only what you have to say; you write only to them; they can infer something about your character only from your writing. So in fewer words,

> Keep in mind that your readers will infer from your style something about your character.

This kind of redundancy often extends through several sentences, each sentence repeating or implying what has already been stated:

> Today, the period in history known as the Holocaust is alive in the interest of many people. Dozens of films have been made, books written, and TV shows produced recording the events that took place during the Holocaust, describing the various aspects of Naziism and the systematic destruction of six million Jews by the Germans under their leader, Adolf Hitler. On the surface, this popular interest in what happened to the Jews under Hitler would appear to be a healthy phenomenon. What could be wrong with a new examination by the media of what is certainly the one single most significant event of twentieth-century history? Unfortunately, this popular interest by so many in the events of the Holocaust has brought with it serious misunderstandings about it, and inevitably incorrect views by those who have been exposed to those misunderstandings.

If we assume that what we say in one sentence doesn't always have to appear in the next, we can make this a good deal leaner and more vigorous:

> Many people have recently become intensely interested in the Holocaust through the dozens of films, books, and TV programs that have dealt with Hitler, Naziism, and the Germans' systematic destruction of six million Jews. On the surface, this interest would appear to be healthy: What could be wrong with reexamining the most significant event of the twentieth century? Unfortunately, this interest has also resulted in some serious misunderstandings.

There is still repetition . . . *this interest* twice. But that repetition provides a consistent sequence of Topics.

Excessive Detail

Other kinds of redundancy are more difficult to prune. Sometimes, we provide irrelevant details.

> Baseball, one of our oldest and most popular outdoor summer sports in terms of total attendance at ball parks and viewing on television, has the kind of rhythm of play on the field that alternates between the players' passively waiting with no action taking place between the pitches to the batter and exploding into action when the batter hits a pitched ball to one of the players and he fields it.

That is,

> Baseball has a rhythm that alternates between waiting and explosive
> action.

How much detail we should provide depends on how much our
readers already know. In technical writing addressed to an informed
audience, we can usually assume a good deal of shared knowledge.

> The basic type results from simple rearrangement of the phonemic con-
> tent of polysyllabic forms so that the initial CV of the first stem syllable
> is transposed with the first CV of the second stem syllable.

The writer didn't bother to define *phonemic content, stem syllable,* or *CV*
because he assumed that anyone reading a technical linguistics journal
would understand those terms.

On the other hand, this definition of *phonetic transcription,* which
would never appear in a technical journal on language, is necessary in an
introductory textbook:

> To study language scientifically, we need some kind of phonetic transcrip-
> tion, a system to write a language so that visual symbols consistently
> represent segments of speech.

A Phrase for a Word

The redundancy we've described so far results when we state what we could
have left implied, a problem we can edit away simply by testing the need
for every word and phrase. But another kind of redundancy is more difficult
to edit away, because to do so we need a precise vocabulary and the wit to
use it. For example,

> As you carefully read what you have written to improve your wording and
> catch small errors of spelling, punctuation, and so on, the thing to do
> before you do anything else is to try to see where sequences of subjects
> and verbs could replace the same ideas expressed in nouns rather than
> verbs.

In other words,

> As you edit, first find nominalizations you can replace with clauses.

We have compressed several words into single words:

carefully read what you have written . . . and so on	=	edit
the thing to do before you do anything else	=	first
try to see where . . . are	=	find
sequences of subjects and verbs	=	clauses
the same ideas expressed in nouns rather than verbs	=	nominalizations

There are no general rules to tell you when you can compress several words into a word or two. I can only point out that you often can and that you should be on the alert for opportunities to do so—try, that is.

You can compress many common phrases:

the reason for for the reason that due to the fact that owing to the fact that in light of the fact that considering the fact that on the grounds that this is why	because, since, why

It is difficult to explain *the reason for* the delay in the completion of the investigation.
It is difficult to explain *why*. . . .

In light of the fact that no profits were reported from 1967 through 1974, the stock values remained largely unchanged.
Because no profits were reported . . .

despite the fact that regardless of the fact that notwithstanding the fact that	although, even though

Despite the fact that the results were checked several times, serious errors crept into the findings.
Even though the results . . .

in the event that if it should transpire/happen that under circumstances in which	if

In the event that the materials arrive after the scheduled date, contact the shipping department immediately.
If the materials arrive . . .

on the occasion of		
in a situation in which	}	when
under circumstances in which		

In a situation in which a class is overenrolled, you may request that the instructor reopen the class.
When a class is overenrolled, . . .

as regards		
in reference to		
with regard to	}	about
concerning the matter of		
where _____ is concerned		

I should now like to make a few observations *concerning the matter of* contingency funds.
I should now like to make a few observations *about* contingency funds.

it is crucial that		
it is necessary that		
there is a need/necessity for	}	must, should
it is important that		
it is incumbent upon		
cannot be avoided		

There is a need for more careful inspection of all welds.
You *must* inspect all welds more carefully.
Inspect all welds more carefully.

It is important that the proposed North-South Thruway not displace significant numbers of residents.
The proposed North-South Thruway *must* not displace significant numbers of residents.

is able to		
is in a position to		
has the opportunity to	}	can
has the capacity for		
has the ability to		

We *are in a position to* make you a firm offer for your house.
We *can* make you a firm offer for your house.

it is possible that
there is a chance that   } may, might, can, could
it could happen that
the possibility exists for

It is possible that nothing will come of these preparations.
Nothing *may* come of these preparations.

prior to
in anticipation of
subsequent to   } before, after, as
following on
at the same time as
simultaneously with

Prior to the expiration of the apprenticeship period, it is incumbent upon you to make application for full membership.
Before your apprenticeship expires, apply for full membership.

increase   } more, less/fewer; better, worse
decrease

There has been an *increase* in the number of universities offering adult education programs.
More universities are offering adult education programs.

We have noted a *decrease* in the quality of applicants.
We have noted that applicants are *less* qualified.

Exercise 5–2

Edit these sentences into more economical form.

1. The future of those engaged in studies at the graduate school level, seeking advanced degrees from institutions of higher education, in regard to prospects for desirable employment in teaching positions at best does not have a high degree of certainty.
2. Notwithstanding the fact that all legal restrictions on the use of

firearms are the subject of heated debate and argument, it is necessary that the general public not stop carrying on discussion pro and con in regard to them.

3.   Under those circumstances in which individuals with financial resources to invest for a profitable return anticipate the possibility that the continually rising prices of things we buy may continue at steadily increasing rates, those individuals will ordinarily put their financial resources into specific objects of artistic value and worth.

4.   In the event that governors of the various states in the United States have the opportunity at some time to get together and talk over with one another the matter of economic needs and problems in their respective states, it is possible that they will find a way to overcome the major problem they have of specifying exactly how to divide up and then distribute Federal economic resources to their different states.

5.   The major matter I want to ask about at this point is the degree to which the consciousness writers have about the individuals they create in their plays puts a disguise on the social tensions of the times in which they are writing.

6.   Those engaged in the profession of education and teaching have for a long period of time been interested in having a better idea about significant improvements in how different individuals learn and commit to memory information from given written textual material. The first matter of difficulty is identifying aspects of common and different features among comparable stretches of writing. The second addresses the difficult matter of assigning some kind of value to the amount of and nature of information that a reader does not forget after that person reads a passage.

TALKING TO THE READER: METADISCOURSE

In Lesson 2, we described **metadiscourse** as the language we use when we refer to our own thinking and writing as we think and write—*to summarize, on the contrary, I believe;* to the structure of what we write—*first, second, more importantly,* etc.; and to our readers's act of reading—*note that, consider now, in order to understand.* We use metadiscourse in personal narratives, arguments, memoirs—in any discourse in which we filter our ideas through a concern with how our reader will take them. Except for numbers to indicate sections and so on, other kinds of writing—operating instructions, technical manuals, laws, and the like—have less metadiscourse.

The problem is to recognize when metadiscourse is useful and then to control it. Some writers use so much metadiscourse that they bury their ideas. For example:

> The last point I would like to make here is that in regard to men-women relationships, it is important to keep in mind that the greatest changes have in all probability occurred in the way men and women seem to be working next to one another.

Only part of that sentence addresses men-women relationships:

> . . . men-women relationships . . . greatest changes have . . . occurred in the way men and women . . . working next to one another.

The rest tells readers how to understand what they are reading:

> The last point I would like to make here is that in regard to . . . it is important to keep in mind that . . . in all probability . . . seem to . . .

Pruned of the writing about reading, the sentence becomes more direct:

> The greatest changes in men-women relationships have occurred in the way men and women work next to one another.

And now that we can see what this sentence really says, we can make it even more direct:

> Men and women have changed their relationships most in the way they work together.

In deciding how much metadiscourse to include, we can't rely on broad generalizations. Some entirely successful writers use a good deal of metadiscourse; others equally successful, very little. More often than not, though, we can reduce it. Read widely in your field with an eye to how writers you think are clear, concise, and successful use metadiscourse. Then do as they do.

Here are some of the more common types of metadiscourse.

Hedges and Emphatics

Each profession has its own idiom of caution and confidence. None of us wants to sound like an uncertain milquetoast or a smug dogmatist. How successfully we walk the rhetorical line between seeming timidity and arrogance depends a good deal on how we manage phrases like *a good deal,* a phrase that a few words ago allowed me to pull back from the more absolute statement:

> How successfully we walk the rhetorical line between seeming timidity and arrogance depends on how we manage phrases like *a good deal.*

Hedges let us sound small notes of civilized diffidence. They give us room to backpedal and to make exceptions. An appropriate emphatic, on the other hand, lets us underscore what we really believe—or would like our reader to think we believe.

Some of the more common hedges: *usually, often, sometimes, almost, virtually, possibly, perhaps, apparently, seemingly, in some ways, to a certain extent, sort of, somewhat, more or less, for the most part, for all intents and purposes, in some respects, in my opinion at least, may, might, can, could, seem, tend, try, attempt, seek, hope.* Some of us use these so often that they become less hedges than meaningless modifiers.

Some of the more common emphatics: *as everyone knows, it is generally agreed that, it is quite true that, it's clear that, it is obvious that, the fact is, as we can plainly see, literally, clearly, obviously, undoubtedly, certainly, of course, indeed, inevitably, very, invariably, always, key, central, crucial, basic, fundamental, major, cardinal, primary, principal, essential.* Words and phrases like these generally mean not much more than "believe me." Used to excess, they sound arrogant or at least defensive. Or they become a kind of background static that robs a style of any clarity or precision. This is another case where a good ear will serve you better than a flat rule. In general, though, hedges and emphatics should be used sparingly.

Sequencers and Topicalizers

Sequencers and topicalizers are words, and phrases, sentences that lead your reader through your text. The least useful kind of sequencers are overelaborate introductions:

> In this next section of this report, it is my intention to deal with the problem of noise pollution. The first thing I want to say is that noise pollution is . . .

You can announce the topic of a whole discourse—or any of its parts—and hint at the structure of its argument more simply:

> The next problem is noise pollution. It . . .

Unless your paper is so complex that you have to lay out its plan in an elaborate introduction, assume that just naming the problem is sufficient to announce it as your topic, and that naming its parts suggests your organization.

Specific topicalizers focus attention on a particular phrase as the main Topic of a sentence, paragraph, or whole section:

> In regard to a *vigorous style,* the most important feature is a short, concrete subject followed by a forceful verb.

> So far as the *industrial development of China* is concerned, it will be years before it can compete with Japan's.

> As to the matter of *responsibility for security,* that is the problem of the staff.

We use phrases and clauses such as *in regard to, where X is concerned, in the matter of, as for, as to, speaking of, turning now to* to announce that we are moving on to a new idea. Better: try to maneuver that new idea into the body of the sentence. For a vigorous style, use a short, concrete subject followed by a forceful verb.

> It will be years before China's *industrialization* can compete with Japan's.

> *Responsibility for security* belongs to the staff.

Probably the most common way we announce prospective Topics is with *there is/are.*

> *There are* three reasons why we should recognize Outer Mongolia.

There is/are often occurs at the beginning of a section, announcing in the phrase that follows *is/are* the topic of that section. But whatever follows *there is/are* is always a static noun phrase. So use this construction only when that phrase is important enough to develop in the next few sentences, or significant enough to assert its existence.

Attributors and Narrators

Attributors and narrators tell your reader where you got your ideas or facts or opinions. Sometimes, when we are still trying to work out precisely what it is we want to say, we offer a narrative of our thinking rather than its results:

> *I was concerned with* the structural integrity of the roof supports, so *I attempted* to test the weight that the transverse beams would carry. *I have concluded* after numerous tests that the beams are sufficiently strong to carry the prescribed weight, but no more. *I think* that it is important that we notify every section that uses the facility of this finding.

If we eliminate the narrators and refocus attention on what the reader needs to know, we make the passage more pointed:

> We must notify every section that uses the storage facility that they must not exceed the prescribed kilogram-per-square-meter floor weight. Tests have established the structural integrity of the transverse beams. They are strong enough to carry the prescribed weights but no more.

Unless your subject matter is the *way* you arrived at your observations or conclusion, you can usually be more concise and direct if you simply present the most salient observations and conclusions, minus the metadiscourse or narrative.

Some writers slip anonymous attribution into their prose by stating that something has been *observed* to exist, is *found* to exist, is *seen, noticed, noted, remarked,* etc.

> High divorce rates *have been observed to occur* in parts of the Northeast that *have been determined to have* especially low population densities.

> Regular patterns of drought and precipitation *have been found to coincide* with cycles of sunspot activity.

Unless you have some good reason to hedge a bit, leave out the fact that any unspecified observor has *observed, found, noticed,* or *seen* something. Just state that it is:

High divorce rates *occur* in parts of the Northeast that *have* especially low population densities.

Regular patterns of drought and precipitation *coincide* with cycles of sunspot activity.

If this seems too flat-footed, drop in a hedge: . . . *apparently coincide.*

Exercise 5-3

In these next sentences, edit for both unnecessary metadiscourse and redundancy.

1. But on the other hand, however, we can point out that it appears that there is going to be TV programming that will on the whole appeal to what can only be considered our most prurient and, therefore, lowest interests.

2. A definition of the term *seborrhea* may be formulated in the following general way: By *seborrhea* we basically refer to an accumulation and buildup on the surface area of the skin of what would be diagnosed as abnormal or unusual sebacious secreted matter, with creation of scab formations or encrustations.

3. It may possibly turn out to be the case that the playwright known to us by the name of William Shakespeare could be someone else, perhaps someone whom we would find to be a member of royalty.

4. In this particular section, I intend to discuss my feelings about the need not to continue with the old approach to plea bargaining. I believe this is the case because of two basic reasons. The first reason that it is necessary to deal with plea bargaining is that it appears to let hardened criminals not receive their just punishment. The second reason is the following: Plea bargaining virtually always encourages a growing lack of respect for the judicial system.

5. In conclusion, I would like to point out that in regard to China, it appears to be a good example of a country on the verge of what many observers agree is going to be what could only be called a major industrial expansion.

6. Turning now to the next question to be discussed, there are in regard to the subject of wild area preservation activities three basic principles when attempting to formulate a way of approaching decisions as to those wild and uninhabited areas unspoiled by human activity that

should be set aside and preserved and not developed for commercial exploitation or business enterprises.

7. It is my underlying belief that in regard to terrestrial-type snakes, the assumption can be made that there are in all probability none to speak of in those unmapped areas of the world not yet explored that would be in excess of the size of those we already have knowledge of.

8. As far as I am concerned, I think that in light of the fact that Leon Trotsky was clearly and distinctly in favor of the Communist Revolution and overthrow of the Tsar, there is no possibility of arguing that he would ever have an objective viewpoint in regard to those events.

9. Depending on the particular view or position that one takes on this question now before us, the family unit and a range of other social institutions that exist in society take on a degree of importance equal to or perhaps even exceeding the aforementioned educational system as a source for the transmission of social values.

10. As we can see, I think that in regard to the current interest in life stages, it would appear that most investigators into the area have a tendency to take the position that the midlife crisis is the most critical period or stage in a person's life development from a mental health point of view; that is to say, we are in a position to know that, for the most part, a large number of us seem to come to the decision at that particular time in our lives whether or not we are going to be on the winning or losing side of the game of life.

NOT THE NEGATIVE

For all practical purposes, these two sentences mean about the same thing:

Don't write in the negative.
Write in the affirmative.

But if we want to be more concise and direct, we should prefer:

Write in the affirmative.

To understand some negatives, we have to translate them into affirmatives, because the negative may only imply what we should do by telling us what we shouldn't do. The affirmative states it directly. Compare what you just read with this:

> "Don't write in the negative" and "Write in the affirmative" *do not mean*
> different things. But if *we don't want* to be indirect, then we *should not*
> *prefer* "Don't write in the negative." *We don't have to translate* an affir-
> mative statement *in order not to misunderstand* it because it *does not*
> *imply* what we should do.

We can't translate every negative sentence into an affirmative. But we can
rephrase many negatives as affirmatives, and unless you have some special
reason to emphasize a *not, no,* or *never,* look for that affirmative sentence.

Some negatives allow almost formulaic translations into affirmatives:

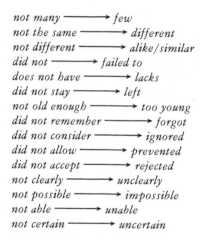

not many ⟶ *few*
not the same ⟶ *different*
not different ⟶ *alike/similar*
did not ⟶ *failed to*
does not have ⟶ *lacks*
did not stay ⟶ *left*
not old enough ⟶ *too young*
did not remember ⟶ *forgot*
did not consider ⟶ *ignored*
did not allow ⟶ *prevented*
did not accept ⟶ *rejected*
not clearly ⟶ *unclearly*
not possible ⟶ *impossible*
not able ⟶ *unable*
not certain ⟶ *uncertain*

Now certainly this advice does not apply to those sentences that raise
an issue by contradicting or denying some point that we intend to correct
(as this sentence demonstrates). One of the most common ways we
introduce discourse is to deny, to say "not so" to someone else's idea of the
truth, or even some possible truth. Once we deny it, we then go on to assert
the truth as we see it:

> In the last decade of the 20th century, we will not find within our own
> borders sufficient oil to meet our needs, nor will we find it in the world
> market. The only way we will increase our oil supply is by developing the
> one resource that we have so far ignored: massive conservation.

When you combine negatives with passives, nominalizations, and
compounds in sentences that are already a bit complex, your writing can
become opaque:

Disengagement of the gears is not possible without locking mechanism release.

Payments should not be forwarded if there has not been due notification of this office.

These negatives all involve two events, one a precondition of the other. We can almost always recast such negatives into more direct affirmatives if we change nominalizations into clauses and passives into actives.

To disengage the gears, first release the locking mechanism.

Before you forward any payments, notify this office.

Which you put first—the outcome or the condition—depends on what the reader already knows, or what the reader is looking for. For example, if you are trying to explain how to reach some known objective, acquire some desired object, put that first:

Except when applicants have submitted applications without appropriate documentation, **benefits** will not be denied.

In this case, we can assume the reader is looking for benefits. Then we put that first, but in the affirmative:

You will receive benefits if you submit appropriate documents.

Or:

To receive benefits, submit appropriate documents.

As you can see from this example, it is especially important to avoid using negatives along with implicitly negative verbs and connecting words such as these:

verbs: **preclude, prevent, lack, fail, doubt, reject, avoid; deny, refuse, exclude, contradict, prohibit, bar,** etc.
conjunctions: **except, unless, provided, however; without, against, lacking, absent, but for.**

One almost formulaic translation involves the words *unless, except,* and *without,* three favorite words when we want to stipulate conditions to an action. We often put the conditional action in the negative, and then introduce the conditions that make it possible with *unless, without,* or *except:*

> **No** provision of this agreement will be waived **unless** done in writing by either party.

The action that is conditioned is a waiver. While we might want to emphasize the importance of *not* doing something, we are ordinarily more concerned about how *to* do something. So we ought to express that action in the affirmative:

> If either party wishes to waive any provision of this agreement, he must do so in writing.

The translation almost always works:

> X may not do Y unless/except/without doing Z.

> ———→ *X may do Y only if X does Z.*

> ———→ *In order to do Y, X must do Z.*

Exercise 5-4

Where appropriate, change the following to affirmatives. Do any additional editing you think useful.

1. It is not possible to reduce inflationary pressures when the federal government does not reduce its spending.
2. Sufficient research has not been directed to problems of those who cannot see when there are not normal levels of light.
3. Scientists have not agreed on the question of whether the universe is open or closed, a dispute that will not be resolved until the total mass of the universe has been computed with an error of no more than 5 percent.
4. So long as taxpayers do not refuse to pay their taxes, the government will have no difficulty in paying its debts.
5. We have no alternative to developing tar sand, oil shale, and coal as sources of fuel, because we cannot make ourselves energy independent without those sources.

6. There has not been adequate carcinogen prevention established in the chemical additive area of meat production.

7. Cancerous tumor treatment is not effective if growth removal is not accomplished before tumor metastasis.

8. Not until a resolution between Catholics and Protestants in regard to papal authority supremacy is achieved will there be the beginning of a reconciliation between the two.

9. Elections in which there is no attempt at dealing with those issues which do not receive adequate attention during the time when no election campaigns are under way cannot serve the functions for which they were intended.

10. The Insured may not refuse to provide the Insurer with all relevant receipts, checks, or other evidence of costs except when such expenses do not exceed $110.

11. Do not discontinue medication unless symptoms of dizziness and nausea fail to alleviate within six hours.

12. The lack of disconfirming evidence suggests that the results are not open to dispute, unless the absence of data from other investigations is taken as a negative factor.

13. No one is precluded from participating in the cost-sharing educational programs without a full hearing into the reasons for his or her rejection.

14. Because there have been no violations of the guidelines by HHS-supported public agencies, there appears to be no reason for the rejection of their application. The conclusion that such action was a result of political pressure cannot be avoided.

Exercise 5-5

Edit the redundancy out of these sentences. Where appropriate change negatives to affirmatives.

1. It seems to me that in a systematic look at the nature of advertising, it is not illogical to start out with a statement that will define the term. This will establish a common point of reference so that we will not be subjective in our approach to a subject matter that is not often the topic of unemotional discussion. Unfortunately there is no single definition for the word *advertising,* making the chances for possible

objectivity not likely. This indicates that the generally popular notions about advertising cannot be examined carelessly.

2. Regardless of the fact that we do not know for certain whether or not there is any possibility of the existence of what we define as life forms in different parts of the universe other than the one in which we exist, it seems probable that evidence that cannot be refuted that is of a basically statistical nature makes it highly unlikely that life could not be found in a large number of planetary systems around tens of thousands of stars scattered throughout the length and the breadth of the universe as we know it.

SUMMING UP
Cutting Fat

You can cut verbal fat if you get rid of the kind of abstraction discussed in Lesson Two. But you can also make your style leaner and more direct if you clear away the more diffuse kind of wordiness we've discussed in this Lesson. Unfortunately, I can't offer any strong generalizations to equal those I suggested about making subjects coincide with agents, verbs with actions, about old information first and new information last. Diffuse wordiness is like a chronic accumulation of specks and motes that individually seem trivial but together blur what might otherwise be a clear and concise style.

Here is a list of major sources of wordiness, along with examples and revisions.

1. *Redundant pairs*

    If and when we can define and establish our final aims and goals, each and every member of our group will be ready and willing to offer aid and assistance.
    If we can define our goals, every member of our group will be ready to help.

2. *Redundant modifiers*

    In this world of today, official governmental red tape is seriously destroying initiative among individual business executives.
    Today, government red tape is destroying initiative among business executives.

3. *Redundant categories*

   In the area of educational activities, tight financial conditions are forcing school board members to cut back in nonessential areas in a drastic manner.
   In education, tight finances are forcing school boards to cut back drastically on nonessentials.

4. *Meaningless modifiers*

   Most students generally find some kind of summer work.
   Most students find summer work.

5. *Obvious implications*

   Energy used to power our industries and homes will in the years to come be increasingly expensive in terms of dollars and cents.
   In the future, energy will cost more.

6. *Pompous diction*

   You must endeavor to facilitate their cognizance of the deleterious result of excessive sesquipedalianism.
   You have to help them realize that big words can have bad results.

7. *Excessive detail*

   A microwave oven that you might buy in any department store uses less energy that is so expensive than a conventional oven that uses gas or electricity.
   Microwave ovens use less energy than conventional ovens.

8. *A phrase for a word*

   A small sail-powered craft that has turned on its side or completely over must remain buoyant enough so that it will bear the weight of those individuals who were aboard.
   A small sailboat that capsizes must float well enough to support its crew.

9. *Excessive metadiscourse*

   It is almost certainly the case that, for the most part, totalitarian systems cannot allow a society to settle into what we would perceive to be stable modes of behavior or, even more crucially perhaps, stable relationships.

> Totalitarian systems cannot allow a society to settle into stable behavior or stable relationships.

10. *Indirect negatives*

> There is no reason not to believe that engineering malfunctions in nuclear energy systems cannot always be anticipated.
> We can assume that malfunctions in nuclear energy systems will surprise us.

You don't have to memorize these types of redundancy, or even unfailingly distinguish one from another. What is important is an eye—or an ear—for a loose phrase, for a useless modifier, for that haze of wordiness that can afflict the prose of even the best writers.

Controlling Sprawl

Too much noise deafens us; too much light dazzles us; too much distance or too much proximity impedes vision; too much length or too much brevity of discourse obscures it....
BLAISE PASCAL

All length is torture....
WILLIAM SHAKESPEARE,
ANTONY AND CLEOPATRA, 4.14

Too much of a good thing is worse than none at all.
ENGLISH PROVERB

What is written without effort is in general read without pleasure.
SAMUEL JOHNSON

O nce you've arranged your ideas, matched their structure to the structure of your sentence, and squeezed out the fat, you have probably also solved the problem of formless, garrulous sentences, of disorganized sprawl. But sometimes, even when you've expressed your ideas directly and economically, you can still lose a reader if you've packed too many ideas into a single sentence.

> Now that the flower children of the '60s and '70s have grown up to become the industrial and service workers of the '80s, employers have discovered that they must learn how to motivate a new kind of worker, who rejects the values of older workers, for whom a job is a means to achieve status and affluence, and instead looks upon labor as a necessary evil that he will endure only if he receives a high salary, generous fringe benefits, and several weeks of paid vacation.

The agents and actions are clear enough. And there is relatively little deadwood. But the sentence is too long to be clear, and, worse, it swallows up its point. For the sake of *my* point, let's agree that the point of this sentence is that employers have to learn to motivate a new kind of worker, an idea stated in the third and fourth lines and simply elaborated on by the rest of the sentence.

Given what we've learned about problems of topic and stress, we can see that the problem with a long sentence may involve more than just garrulousness. When you add clause after clause to a sentence, you are obscuring those signals that make discourse coherent and emphatic. A long sentence lets you signal your topic prominently only once: at the beginning. And it lets you signal emphasis prominently only once: at the end. You risk letting everything else get sucked up into a formless muddle in the middle, including what may be the *main* point of the sentence.

Compare this:

> Now that the flower children of the '60s and '70s have grown up to become the industrial and service workers of the '80s, employers have discovered that they must learn how to motivate a new kind of worker. These young employees have rejected the values of older workers, for whom a job was a means to achieve status and affluence. Instead, they look upon labor as a necessary evil that they will endure only if they receive high salaries, generous fringe benefits, and several weeks of paid vacation.

The passage now has a topic string that more clearly directs the reader through its ideas: *the flower children, employers, These young employees, they.* And perhaps more important, the point of the passage is now emphasized in its own sentence, whose own stress emphasizes the new information. Then the two succeeding sentences appropriately emphasize their most important ideas:

> . . . rejected the value of older workers
>   . . . a means to achieve status and affluence.
> . . . labor as a necessary evil
>   . . . high salaries, generous fringe benefits, and several weeks of
>   paid vacation.

Notice too that, if we wished, we could now move that point sentence to the end of its passage, for a more dramatic effect:

> The flower children of the '60s and '70s have now grown up to
> become the industrial and service workers of the '80s. They reject
> the values of older workers, for whom a job was a means to achieve
> status and affluence, and instead look upon labor as a necessary evil
> that they will endure only if they receive high salaries, generous
> fringe benefits, and several weeks of paid vacations. Employers
> have discovered that they must now learn how to motivate this
> new kind of worker.

TWO KINDS OF LONG SENTENCES

We have to distinguish two kinds of long sentences; the one you're reading right now, for example, is rather long, sixty-three words to be exact, but it's long simply because I have chosen to punctuate what might have been a series of shorter sentences as one long sentence; those semicolons could have been periods—and that dash could have been one too.

I can write a different kind of sentence just as long as that but one that doesn't let me trade a comma, semicolon, or dash for a period, because it is made up of several subordinate parts, all of them depending on a single main clause—a sentence such as the one you are now reading, which is also exactly sixty-three words long.

Both of those sentences are single **punctuated sentences**, strings of words that begin with a capital letter and end with a period. But the first consists of shorter sentence segments, shorter coordinated clauses, each of which could have been punctuated as a separate sentence, as in this slightly revised version:

> We have to distinguish two kinds of long sentences. The one you're read-ing right now, however, is rather short, sixteen words to be exact. But it's short because I have simply chosen to punctuate what might have been one long sentence as a series of shorter ones. Those periods could have been semicolons. And that last period could have been a dash.

Traditionally, we use the term *compound sentence* to describe a punctuated sentence in which we link clause to clause with semicolons or with coordinating conjunctions such as *and, but, yet, for, so, or,* or *nor.* More than two or three such clauses in a single punctuated sentence risks a tumbling of ideas:

> Language was one of the great evolutionary breakthroughs in our species, *and* it probably made possible the domination of a large food-providing area by a relatively few creatures, *and* it may even have enhanced selec-tion for intellectual power, *but* without the equally important ability to use tools, we never would have survived, *so* it is important that we analyze our evolution in both these contexts, *and* that is what this chapter will do.

Even though that is a very long punctuated sentence, it consists of several short and simple **grammatical sentences.** A grammatical sentence is a sentence that we *cannot* break into shorter sentences with just a period, no matter how long it is. Traditionally, we call these either *simple sen-tences,* sentences with a single clause:

> The source of certain knowledge always puzzled Socrates.

or *complex sentences,* sentences with an independent clause and at least one subordinate clause:

> [Although there are many great dictionaries,] the greatest dictionary of them all is the *Oxford English Dictionary.*

Keep this principle in mind: If a very long *punctuated* sentence is also a single *grammatical* sentence, it may be difficult to read because it gives a reader no place to pause and begin again. On the other hand, if a very long punctuated sentence consists of several short grammatical sentences, it may be simple to read, but it may also sound a bit immature.

THE BEST LENGTH

We can decide how long a sentence ought to be in two ways. First, we could aim at a statistical norm for different kinds of prose. In ordinary magazine writing, for example, sentences average about twenty to twenty-two words. In more technical and academic prose, they are longer. In writing aimed at a general reading public, newspaper writing for example, sentences are shorter.

The better way to think about length is to develop an eye—or ear—for when a sentence runs on too long. In practice, a grammatical sentence usually becomes too long when a writer tacks on to one clause another that modifies it, and to that clause, yet one more:

> The function of myth is to tell a story *that* will allow an interpretation *that* speaks to some problem basic to the society of its audience *because* myth is a kind of history *that* orders the world for preliterates for *whom* abstract moral or social philosophy would be irrelevant

That's the second kind of sprawl: not several sentences within a single punctuated sentence, but a single grammatical sentence that wanders through one tacked-on clause after another.

As a first step toward sensing when your sentences begin to sprawl, find out roughly how long they run./The easiest way to find out is to put a slash at every period and inside every punctuated sentence where a grammatical sentence ends;/a grammatical sentence ended there, for example,/and another ends here./If you know roughly how many words a line of your typed or written copy averages—usually ten to fourteen—then you can tell at a glance roughly how many words you average per sentence./Since that one ran about three typed lines, I guess it was about thirty-three to thirty-six words long, close enough for our purposes.

If most of your sentences run more than two-and-a-half or three lines, you may be plain wordy, or you may be trying to pack too much into your sentences. And in so doing, you may be expecting too much of your readers.

CUTTING DOWN LONG SENTENCES

The simplest way to edit sprawling sentences, particularly long punctuated sentences with lots of *ands* or *buts,* is simply to stop them with a period and delete the unnecessary conjunctions. Compare this with the original version on page 110.

> Language was one of the great evolutionary breakthroughs in our species: It probably made possible the domination of a large food-providing area by a relatively few creatures; it may even have enhanced selection for intellectual power. But without the equally important ability to use tools, we never would have survived. It is important that we analyze our evolution in both these contexts. That is what this chapter will do.

You can usually drop *and* because *and* usually just means "Here's one more thing." You can also drop most *so* s. If you find that you can't, the flow of your argument may need some attention: Logical conclusions should be obvious from what preceded them.

Ordinarily, you can't omit a *but* or *yet* because readers have to know right away if you are contradicting something they just read. When we remove the *but,* the sentence beginning with *Without* seems disjointed:

> Language was one of the great evolutionary breakthroughs in our species: It probably made possible the domination of a large food-providing area by a relatively few creatures; it may even have enhanced selection for intellectual power. Without the equally important ability to use tools, we never would have survived. It is important that we analyze our evolution in both these contexts. That is what this chapter will do.

As a general rule, if a clause beginning with *but* or *and* introduces a major point that you intend to develop, punctuate that clause as a separate sentence:

> We must acknowledge that the United States government has a history of broken treaties with the Indian nations that trusted it, *but it is equally true* that in recent history, our government has attempted to redress many of those broken agreements. In Maine, for example, the federal government has. . . .

If you begin a new sentence at *But it is equally true,* you make the thesis more prominent:

> We must acknowledge that the United States government has a history of broken treaties with the Indian nations that trusted it. *But it is equally true* that in recent history, our government has attempted to redress many of those broken agreements. In Maine, for example, . . .

When the clauses are short and the *but-* clause is closely tied to the preceding clause, split them with a period only if you want to give that second clause special emphasis:

> Prices are going up, *but* wages are not.
> Prices are going up. *But* wages are not.

While you can simply repunctuate a long sentence, made up of several grammatical sentences, you have to rewrite a bit when you split up a single long grammatical sentence. Here are some ways to do it.

Splitting before an *And*

If the sentence consists of long coordinate verb phrases, stop before the *and* or *but* and find subjects for the second verb.

> Students of animal behavior *have been concerned* with the problem of the sensory control of motivation and emotion during periods of unusual stress *and have studied* the behavior of many species under controlled conditions of various kinds.

> Students of animal behavior *have been concerned* with the problem of the sensory control of motivation and emotion during periods of unusual stress. *They have studied* the behavior of many species under controlled conditions of various kinds.

Splitting before *although/because/if*

To split a sentence before a subordinating conjunction, we first have to turn a subordinate clause into an independent clause. The most convenient way to start is by breaking a long sentence just before or after a dependent clause beginning with *although, because, if* and so on. You then have to replace that *although, because, if* with a new sentence connector.

1. *although, though, while* ⟶ *but, yet, however. Although* and *but* signal qualifications in different ways. When we read a sentence that begins with *although,* we are warned to keep in mind that the

first idea is going to be contradicted by what follows. But (as in this case) when the contradiction is signaled by *but* or *however,* we have to recall the previous sentence in order to qualify it.

Although the court ordered the police to remain on the job until the injunction against the strike had been set aside by a higher court, they refused the order and went out on strike regardless of the penalties that they knew would be levied against them.

The court ordered the police to remain on the job . . . set aside by a higher court. **But** they refused the order and went out on strike. . . .

This is one reason why you want to put *however, on the other hand,* and so on close to the beginning of their sentences. When you signal your contradiction at the end of a sentence, you force your reader to go back *two* full sentences to make sense out of the pair:

Legalized gambling is a potentially rich source of tax revenue for traditionally underfinanced areas of public administration. In most places where gambling has been legalized, it has proven to be a source of serious social problems, **however.**

If the writer had put the *however* earlier, the reader would not have to backtrack:

. . . areas of public administration. In most places where gambling has been legalized, **however,** it has proven . . .

2.   *because, since,* ———⟶ *as a result, consequently, for, so, because of this.* Somewhat more complicated is how you split cause-and-effect sentences linked with *because* or *since.* When the *because-* clause comes first, you can start the second sentence with *as a result, consequently,* and so on. Avoid *this had the result of, this resulted in, this led to,* or *this had the effect of,* because the prepositions at the end of those phrases will force you into awkward nominalizations:

Because the soaring cost of energy, the most important factor in the world economy of the late twentieth century, has shaken the confidence of the world in the industrialized nations' ability to sustain a healthy rate of growth, *fewer economists predict* that the less developed nations can look forward to a reasonably promising future.

The soaring cost of energy, the most important factor in the world economy of the late twentieth century, has shaken the confidence of the world in the industrialized nations' ability to sustain a healthy rate of growth. **This development has resulted in** *fewer predictions by economists* that the less developed nations can look forward to a reasonably promising future.

Compare the awkward nominalization, *resulted in* **fewer predictions by economists,** with the more direct subject-verb that follows *as a result, consequently,* or even *because of this:*

. . . ability to sustain a healthy rate of growth. **As a result,** *fewer economists predict* that the less developed nations. . . .

It is more difficult to split a sentence between a main clause and a following subordinate clause that begins with *because.* English has no idiomatic connective parallel to *therefore* or *as a result* to signal that the second clause is a cause. Occasionally, *for* will serve:

Many of our older cities are facing fiscal crises far worse than any they have thus far experienced. **For** facilities that were built years ago are deteriorating and will have to be completely replaced in the not-too-distant future.

But *for* is weak, a bit formal, and it signals logical rather than causal consequences. It won't do for long, complex sentences about complex causes. There are other introductions, but four of them end in prepositions that force us into muddy nominalizations. Don't begin sentences with *this was caused by/resulted from/was owing to/was due to:*

. . . crises that are far worse than any they have thus far experienced. **This crisis is due to** *the deterioration of facilities* that were built years ago. . . .

Compare the slightly longer but more direct subject-verb clause:

. . . crises that are far worse than any they have thus far experienced. **This crisis has occurred because** *facilities that were built years ago have deteriorated* and will need . . .

3.   *if, provided that,* ──────▶ *if so, if this happens.* Just as English lacks a graceful connecting word to signal the cause of something stated in a

preceding sentence, it also lacks a graceful connecting word that would signal a reader that a second sentence asserts the condition for what a first sentence has asserted as a consequent.
Compare:

If demographic changes continue as they have over the last several years, shrinking the population by as much as 25 percent, *we may find it difficult* to go on supporting a large elderly population on the taxed earnings of a relatively small labor force.

We have to invent a new subject and verb just to introduce the consequent clause:

Over the last several years, demographic changes have shrunk the working population by as much as 10 percent. **If that trend continues . . ./If that is so . . .**

The implicitly negative conditionals *unless* and *except(ing) that* sometimes make for difficult reading, especially when they combine with explicit negatives:

The regulation will **no** longer govern this situation, **unless** the Agency does **not** decide to review it.

Avoid negatives in general (see pp. 99–102), but especially with conditionals. You can almost always translate a negative conditional into an affirmative if you delete the negative and change the *unless* to *only if.*

No royalties will be paid **unless** the parties agree.

Royalties will be paid **only if** the parties agree.

How do we decide to put qualifications, causes, or conditions before or after the sentences they qualify? That depends entirely on issues we dealt with in Lessons Three and Four. The principle is a simple one: Whatever you intend to expand on, explain, analyze— put it last.

Although legalized gambling can create serious social problems, it is a rich source of tax revenue. Both Nevada and New Jersey have realized several millions of dollars . . .

If the writer had intended to pick up on the social problems, then the clause referring to them should appear last:

Although legalized gambling is a rich source of tax revenue, it can also create serious social problems. Communities in which such gambling is allowed have experienced sharp increases in prostitution, robbery, loan sharking . . .

If we end a sentence with a clause beginning with *although,* that clause will seem to be a tacked-on afterthought:

Legalized gambling is a rich source of tax revenue, **although** it carries social risks that we might want to avoid.

If you feel you can't rearrange the sentence but you want to emphasize what that *although*-clause signals, then change the *although* to *even though:*

Legalized gambling is a rich source of tax revenues **even though** it carries social risks that we might want to avoid.

Splitting before a *which/who/that-* clause

A string of relative clauses is invariably limp and graceless:

Of all the areas of scientific advancement that are important not just to the future of science but to everyday life on this planet, few have consequences more potentially awesome than genetic engineering **that** manipulates the elemental structures and units of life itself, **which** are the genes and chromosomes **that** direct our cells how to reproduce and become the functional parts of all life forms.

We can correct it by simply cutting the string at some appropriate place.

Of all the areas of scientific advancement that are important not just to the future of science but to everyday life on this planet, few have consequences more potentially awesome than genetic engineering. **Genetic engineering** manipulates the elemental structures and units of life itself. **These** are the genes and chromosomes **that** direct our cells how to reproduce and become the functional parts of all life forms.

When a *which* refers to the whole of the preceding clause, find a subject that will replace the *which* and begin a new sentence.

> Mapmaking in Europe entered a renaissance in both theory and practice during the sixteenth and seventeenth centuries, **which** was the result of exploration and colonization of the New World and commercial relations with Asia.

> Mapmaking in Europe entered a renaissance in both theory and practice during the sixteenth and seventeenth centuries. **This development** resulted from the exploration and colonization of the New World and commercial relations with Asia.

You can also tidy up your longer sentences if in relative clauses you can delete *who/that/which* + *is/are/was,* etc.

> Any assignments **that are** not yet completed will have to be submitted at a time **which will be** designated by the person **who is** responsible for scheduling.

> Any assignments [   ] not yet completed will have to be submitted at a time [   ] designated by the person [   ] responsible for scheduling.

Occasionally you can drop just *that/which/who* but when you do, you'll have to rewrite the verb into a different form.

> Organized labor has lost a good deal of the political power it once used to support programs **that benefitted** rank-and-file workers.

> Organized labor has lost a good deal of the political power it once used to support programs [   ] **benefitting** rank-and-file workers.

> The day is not far off when we will all be assigned numbers **that will identify** every financial transaction so that the government can monitor every area of our lives **that involves** economic activity.

> The day is not far off when we will all be assigned numbers [   ] **identifying** every financial transaction so that the government can monitor every area of our lives [   ] **involving** economic activity.

Splitting with a Colon

If a sentence contains a long list, you can help the reader by introducing it with a colon. But ordinarily, complete the sentence before you introduce the list. The writer of this sentence did not do so.

> In order to analyze the structural properties of discourse it is necessary **to
> account for: the flow** of semantic information in the paragraph; the
> devices used to achieve coherence such as *therefore, and, on the other
> hand;* the repeated words that define the lexical field: and the functional
> units in paragraphs, such as topic sentences.

First, we add whatever words we need to complete the sentence, then
we introduce the list:

> In order to analyze the structural properties of discourse, it is necessary to
> account **for the following: the flow of** semantic information in a para-
> graph, the devices. . . .

(Note: Most handbooks recommend beginning the section after a
colon with a lower-case letter. If what follows the colon is not a complete
clause, begin with the lower-case letter. But if you have finished one clause
and are beginning another complete clause, you can signal that fact by
beginning that next clause with a capital letter: This clause is an example.

Exercise 6-1

All these sentences are too long. Split them into smaller units; then edit
them in the ways we've been discussing.

1. Several activities have already evolved at this college in response to
    the problems identified in the self-study to meet the ever-expanding
    range of student learning desires, styles, and capabilities, and these
    new programs also relate to the traditional goals of the college,
    which include education of the whole person in the basic skills of
    liberal education.
2. Two themes that are not separated in the discussion are: first, the
    apprenticeship nature of graduate medical training, which is there-
    fore at base not a formal process, and, second, teaching competence
    in the three areas of professional learning, including knowledge,
    technique, and behavioral skills and attitudes, which require that
    graduate medical training not exclude formal instruction and work in
    classroom contexts.
3. Regardless of the fact that the training program has a long financial
    problem history and management-staff dispute record because of
    unclear responsibility definition, it is equally true that in the period

of the last few years or so, it has with considerable success placed in the area of 50 percent of its trainees in various different jobs and positions equal to their training and skill-level preparation.

4. Being alone and being lonely are not the same feeling that a person has resulting from how well that person can draw on resources that he or she has developed during the time he or she was growing into adulthood, which is the period in our lives when we all have to face up to who we are and whether we can live with ourselves for the rest of our lives.

5. Many city dwellers find it a necessity to give up on life as it exists in the city at the present time as a consequence of things such as dirt and crime that finally defeat them despite the fact that on the occasion of their leaving for more rural environs, they often come to the realization that they wish they again had the intensity and excitement that makes life in the city such a stimulating experience.

6. An institution or organization that is disappearing from the general business life in this country is known as the men-only club, that seems to have traditionally provided a place where business deals and arrangements could be brought to a conclusion in an atmosphere of an intimately male character, for the reason that increasing numbers of women have no reluctance about exercising a business power and might that once was in the possession only of men and so demand the same amenities and conveniences that once were the privilege of men alone.

7. The underlying basic assumption of this procedure presupposes: a large enough sample size sufficient so that it does not result in the exclusion of a range of variation that we would not be surprised to find in the total population involved, an analysis not in contradiction with accepted statistical methodological procedures, and a replication of the study under conditions which have no significant differences from those that existed in other studies of this kind.

8. Lear experiences a failure in the ability to recognize the faithlessness of Goneril and Regan and the honesty of Cordelia and the Fool and also cannot recognize who the disguised Kent is, who through a kind of flattery that is like that of Lear's faithless daughters creates in Lear the belief that he serves him, for despite the fact that Kent's intentions are of an honorable kind, his flattery of Lear as someone who would be his "master" is a kind of deceit which takes advantage of the vanity of Lear, and even gives encouragement to it.

9. To obligate a corporation upon a contract to another party, it must be proven by the other party that the contract was the act of the corporation, whether by corporate action, that of an authorized agent, or by adoption and ratification by the Board of Directors and such ratification will be implied by the acquiescence or the acceptance of any of the benefits of such contract, it being essential to such implied ratification that the acceptance be with knowledge of all pertinent facts.

10. The Internal Revenue Service in Private Letter Ruling 83–338, in the course of a ruling which concluded that a sale of mortgages between members of an affiliated group filing a consolidated return, followed by their pledge of the mortgages to secure mortgage-backed bonds, was a tax-deferred intercompany transaction, also applied and relied upon Revenue Ruling 76–984 to hold that the use of a wholly-owned subsidiary of the builder-parent to originate the mortgages in the manner contemplated would not cause the builder to be considered by the IRS to have received the purchase price from the purchasers.

SUMMING UP
Controlling Sprawl

Here's a checklist for controlling sprawl.

1. Make an inventory of your sentence length by putting a slash after every punctuated sentence. Put a slash between all grammatical sentences inside punctuated sentences. Check sentences that run more than three or so lines for smaller grammatical sentences.

2. Consider whether two or more grammatical sentences inside a single punctuated sentence might read more clearly or more emphatically if you punctuated them as separate sentences. Look especially carefully at long punctuated sentences that might contain a crucial point expressed in a shorter grammatical sentence. Don't crowd an important point into a long punctuated sentence with other, less important elements. Set it off as a separate, punctuated sentence:

In the 1950s several researchers mapped areas of the brain by stimulating various cortical points with small electrical charges; as different parts of the brain were stimulated, subjects reported verbally the sensations they experienced, and what scientists were astonished to discover was that we can recall from deep inside our brains memories that would otherwise have remained locked away forever.

. . . subjects reported verbally the sensations they experienced. Scientists were astonished to discover that we can recall from deep inside our brains. . . .

3. If a long punctuated sentence does *not* consist of shorter grammatical sentences, consider more extensive rewriting.

   a. If your sentence contains two or more long, coordinate verb phrases after the subject, put a period after the first verb phrase. Then repeat the subject/topic to change the second verb phrase into an independent sentence:

   We first postulated cost-benefit curves for the change-over extending through 1990, taking into consideration the anticipated rate of inflation through that time, **and then projected** a profit ratio to determine whether the investment risk justified our allocating 75 percent of our research efforts in this area.

   . . . the anticipated rate of inflation through that time. **We then projected** a profit ratio. . . .

   b. If your sentence concludes with a long relative clause beginning with a *which* that refers to all that precedes it, replace the *which* with a *this* + noun, and begin a new sentence:

   Increasing numbers of undergraduates are looking to the master's degree in business administration as their passport to financial success and a world of challenge and excitement, **which** reveals how much students have changed from the more politically and socially aware years of the '60s.

   . . . challenge and excitement. **This new interest** reveals how much students have changed from. . . .

   c. If a long sentence concludes with a relative clause, rewrite the relative clause as an independent sentence:

   If those of lower socioeconomic origins decline to participate in these studies and if their economic status is related to the effectiveness of the treatments, then the study will not effectively evaluate the therapy for the nonparticipating group, **which** as a result may undergo a therapy that is not appropriate to their special medical needs.

. . . will not effectively evaluate the therapy for the nonparticipating group. **This group,** as a result, may undergo a therapy that is not appropriate. . . .

d. If your sentence has a long adverbial clause beginning with *because, although, if,* etc., delete the conjunction, end the clause with a period. Then introduce the following sentence with an appropriate sentence connector:

Although in Elizabethan England the rate of inflation was higher than it ever had been or would ever be again for another three centuries, peasants were less affected than we might expect **because** many of them grew their own food, made their own clothing, and relied less on the exchange of coin than on the exchange of kind.

In Elizabethan England the rate of inflation was higher than it ever had been or would ever be again for another three centuries. **But** peasants were less affected than we might expect: Many of them grew their own food . . .

(Note that we replaced an initial *although* with a subsequent *but* and substituted a colon for a *because.*)

4. Finally, reread. Make sure that the *order* of the new sentences is appropriate. Be particularly sure that the topic-stress sequence works. Do the sentences have a consistent topic? Does the stress of one sentence lead into the next? And finally, does the central point of the originally long sentence stand out in the way you want it to? Is it worth expressing in a single short sentence? Do you want it to introduce the new string of sentences, or do you want them to lead up to it?

Compare:

Laws that require Plain English are beginning to appear in increasing numbers of states because legislators are beginning to realize that the general public is not well served by guarantees, contracts, patient consent forms, and so on that require an advanced degree to understand, although in many states lawyers are objecting to any changes in the laws at all because they fear either litigation over any new language or the reduced fees that less litigation would bring them.

Laws that require Plain English are beginning to appear in increasing numbers of states. In many states, however, lawyers are objecting to any changes in the laws at all. They fear litigation over any new language. Or they fear the reduced fees that less litigation would bring them. But legislators are beginning to realize that the general public is not well served by guarantees, contracts, patient consent forms, and so on that require an advanced degree to understand.

Legislators are finally beginning to realize that the general public is not well served by guarantees, contracts, patient consent forms, and so on that require an advanced degree to understand. In many states, it is true, lawyers are objecting to any changes in the laws at all. They fear litigation over any new language. Or they fear the reduced fees that less litigation would bring them. But laws requiring Plain English are beginning to appear in increasing numbers of states.

Which of the rewritten versions we prefer would depend on what we want to do with this passage: Are we summing up, introducing, explaining? What impact do we want to achieve? At this point, mechanical rules must yield to judicious choice.

Managing Long Sentences

Sentences in their variety run from simplicity to complexity, a progression not necessarily reflected in length: a long sentence may be extremely simple in construction—indeed must be simple if it is to convey its sense easily.

SIR HERBERT READ

A long complicated sentence should force itself upon you, make you know yourself knowing it. . . .

GERTRUDE STEIN

The ability to write clear, crisp sentences that never go beyond twenty words is a considerable achievement. You'll never confuse a reader with sprawl, wordiness, or muddy abstraction. But if you never write sentences longer than twenty words, you'll be like a pianist who uses only the middle octave: You can carry the tune, but without much variety or range. Every competent writer has to know how to write a concise sentence and how to prune a long one to readable length. But a competent writer must also know how to manage a long sentence gracefully, how to make it as clear and as vigorous as a series of short ones.

Now, several long clauses in a single grammatical sentence do not in themselves constitute formless sprawl. Here is a sentence with eighteen subordinate clauses, seventeen of them leading up to the single main clause and the eighteenth bringing up the end:

> Now if nature should intermit her course and leave altogether, though it were but for a while, the observation of her own laws; if those principal and mother elements of the world, whereof all things in this lower world are made, should lose the qualities which now they have; if the frame of that heavenly arch erected over our heads should loosen and dissolve itself; if celestial spheres should forget their wonted motions, and by irregular volubility turn themselves any way as it might happen; if the prince of the lights of heaven, which now as a giant doth run his unwearied course, should, as it were through a languishing faintness, begin to stand and to rest himself; if the moon should wander from her beaten way, the times and seasons of the year blend themselves by disordered and confused mixture, the winds breathe out their last gasp, the clouds yield no rain, the earth be defeated of heavenly influence, the fruits of the earth pine away as children at the withered breasts of their mother no longer able to yield them relief—what would become of man himself, whom these things now do all serve?
>
> —Thomas Hooker, *Of the Laws of Ecclesiastical Polity,* 1594

Whatever else we may want to say about that sentence, it does not sprawl. Its Ciceronian intricacy may no longer appeal to most modern ears, but its clauses fit together as neatly as the universe Hooker describes. So it is not length alone, or number of clauses alone, that we ought to worry about, but rather long sentences without shape.

Here are a few ways you can extend a sentence and still keep it clear and graceful. The easiest is coordination.

COORDINATION

We can join grammatically equal segments with *and, but, yet* or *or* any-where in a sentence. But we do it most gracefully after the subject, in the predicate. If we create a long subject, our reader has to hold her breath until she gets to the verb. Compare the second sentence in these two passages. The first is Gore Vidal's original account of how the Founding Fathers viewed democracy and monarchy, the other my revision.

> The Inventors of the United States decided that there would be no hereditary titles in God's country. Although the Inventors were hostile to the idea of democracy and believed profoundly in the sacredness of property and the necessary dignity of those who owned it, they did not like the idea of king, duke, marquess, earl.

> The Inventors of the United States decided that there would be no hereditary titles in God's country. Their profound belief in the necessary dignity of those who owned property and in its sacred-ness and a hostility to the idea of democracy did not lead them to like the idea of king, duke, marquess, and earl.

Vidal designed his coordinations so that they all appeared **after** his subject and ordered them so that the shorter elements of the coordinations appeared before the longer ones:

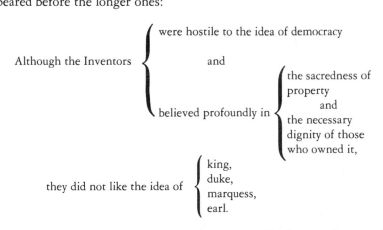

In general, a vigorous sentence moves quickly from a short and specific subject through a strong verb to its complement, where we can, if we wish, more gracefully elaborate our syntax and more fully develop our ideas. So if we extend a sentence by coordinating its parts, we should coordinate after the subject more often than before the verb.

In using coordination to build longer sentences, we have to avoid two problems.

1. *Faulty Parallelism.* When we coordinate sentence parts that have different grammatical structures, we may create an offensive lack of parallelism. A common rule of rhetoric and grammar is that we should coordinate elements only of the same grammatical structure: clause and clause, predicate and predicate, prepositional phrase and prepositional phrase, etc. Most careful writers would avoid this:

These advertisements persuade us
    { that the corporation supports environmentalism
                        but not
      to buy its frivolous products.

Corrected:

. . . persuade us   { *that the corporation supports* environmentalism

                          but not

                        that we should buy its frivolous products.

This also would be considered nonparallel:

The committee recommends   { *completely revising the curriculum in applied education* in order to reflect trends in local employment

                                and

                              that the administrative structure of the division be modified to reflect the new curriculum

Corrected:

... recommends {
*that the curriculum in applied education
be completely revised* in order to reflect
trends in local employment

and

*that the administrative structure of the
division be modified* to reflect the new
curriculum.
}

And yet some nonparallel coordinations occur in well-written prose
fairly often. Writers frequently join a noun phrase with a *how*-clause.

Every attempt will be
made to delineate {
the problems of biomedical education
among the underdeveloped nations

and

how a coordinated effort can address
them in the most economical and
expeditious way.
}

Or an adjective or adverb with a prepositional phrase:

The grant proposal
appears to have been
written {
*intelligently,
carefully,*

and

with the full cooperation of all the
agencies whose interests this project
involves.
}

Some teachers and editors would insist on rewriting these into
parallel form:

... to delineate {
the problems of biomedical education

and

the coordinated effort necessary for the
most economical and expeditious
solution.
}

The grant proposal
appears to have been
written with
$$\left\{ \begin{array}{l} \textit{intelligence,} \\ \textit{care,} \\ \qquad\qquad \textit{and} \\ \textit{the full cooperation of} \ldots \end{array} \right.$$

But most educated readers don't even notice the "faulty" parallelism here, much less find it offensive.

2. *Lost Connections.* What will bother readers more than mildly faulty parallelism is a grammatical coordination so long that they either lose track of its internal connections or, worse, misread them:

> Every teacher ought to remind himself daily that his students are vulnerable people, insecure and uncertain about those everyday, ego-bruising moments that adults no longer concern themselves with, and that they do not understand that one day they will become as confident and as secure as the adults that bruise them.

That momentary flicker of hesitation about where to connect

> . . . and that they do not understand that one day they . . .

is enough to interrupt the flow of the sentence.

To revise a sentence like this, try to shorten the first half of the coordination so that the second half is closer to that point in the sentence where the coordination begins:

> Every teacher ought to remind himself that his students are more vulnerable to those ego-bruising moments that adults have learned to cope with and that those students do not understand that one day . . .

If you can't do that, try repeating a word that will remind the reader where the second half of the coordination begins:

> Every teacher ought **to remind himself that** his students are vulnerable to those ego-bruising moments that adults have learned to cope with, **to remind himself that** those students do not understand that one day . . .

And, of course, you can always begin a new sentence:

> . . . adults no longer concern themselves with. Teachers should remind themselves that their students do not understand . . .

SUBORDINATION

Resumptive Modifiers

A simple device that lets you extend almost any sentence we will call a *resumptive modifier*. Resumptive modification repeats a key noun, verb, or adjective close to the end of a clause and then resumes the line of thought, elaborating on what went before. It is a pattern that lets the reader pause for a moment, then move on.

Compare:

> For several years the Columbia Broadcasting System created and developed situation comedies that were the best that American TV had to offer, such as "The Mary Tyler Moore Show" and "All in the Family" that sparkled with wit and invention.

> For several years, the Columbia Broadcasting System created and developed situation **comedies** that were the best that American TV had to offer,
>> **comedies** such as "The Mary Tyler Moore Show" and "All in the Family,"
>> **comedies** that sparkled with wit and invention.

At best, that first sentence verges on rhythmic monotony. The writer tacked on a relative clause, *comedies that were the best,* and then without a pause a second, *". . . All in the Family that sparkled with wit and invention.* The resumptive modifiers in the revision let us pause for a moment, catch our breath, and then move on.

You can pause and resume with parts of speech other than nouns. Here with adjectives:

> It was American writers who first used a vernacular that was both **true** and **lyrical,**
>> **true** to the rhythms of the working man's speech,
>> **lyrical** in its celebration of the land.

Here with verbs:

> Humans have been defined by some as the only animal that can **laugh** at grief,
>> **laugh** at the pain and tragedy that define their fate.

Summative Modifiers

Somewhat similar is the *summative modifier*. With a summative modifier, you end a segment of a sentence with a comma, then sum up in a noun or noun phrase what you have just said, and then continue with a relative clause.

Compare these:

> In the last five years, European population growth has dropped to almost zero, **which** in years to come will have profound social implications.

> In the last five years, European population growth has dropped to almost zero,
> > **a demographic event that** in years to come will have profound social implications.

> Scientists have finally unraveled the mysteries of the human gene, **which** may lead to the control of such dread diseases as cancer and birth defects.

> Scientists have finally unraveled the mysteries of the human gene,
> > **a discovery that** may lead to the control of such dread diseases as cancer and birth defects.

The summative modifier avoids the gracelessness and the potential ambiguity of a vague *which* and lets the writer extend the line of the sentence without slipping into a drone.

Free Modifiers

A third kind of modifier that lets you extend a sentence and still avoid monotony resembles the previous two but works a bit differently. This modifier follows the verb but comments on its subject. It usually makes more specific what you assert in the preceding clause that you attach it to.

Compare:

> However violent King Kong appeared, he always seemed to work hard at being a noble savage who protected his fair captive against prehistoric monsters and who treated her with the gentleness of an exceptionally hairy and overgrown but basically decent Tarzan.

> However violent King Kong appeared, he always seemed to work hard at being a noble savage,

> **protecting** his fair captive against prehistoric monsters,
> **treating** her with the gentleness of an exceptionally hairy
> and overgrown but basically decent Tarzan.

These free modifiers most often begin with an **-ing** participle:

> The Scopes monkey trial was a watershed in American religious thinking,
> > **legitimizing** the contemporary interpretation of the Bible
> > and
> > **making** literal fundamentalism a backwater of anti-
> > intellectual theology.

But they can also begin with a past participle form of the verb:

> Leonardo da Vinci was a man of powerful intellect,
> > **driven** by an insatiable curiosity and
> > **haunted** by a vision of artistic expression.

Or with an adjective:

> In 1939 the United States began to assist the British in their struggle
> against Germany,
> > **fully aware** that it faced another world war.

Exercise 7-1

In these next sentences, create resumptive, summative, and free modifiers. In the first five, use the word in italics as the start of the resumptive modifier, and use the word in parentheses to start the summative modifier. Then pick four or five sentences and create a free modifier on your own. For example:

> Within ten years, we could meet 25 percent of our energy needs with
> solar *energy*. (a possibility)

Resumptive:

> Within ten years, we could meet 25 percent of our energy needs with
> solar *energy, energy* that is safe, cheap and plentiful.

Summative:

> Within ten years, we could meet 25 percent of our energy needs with solar energy, *a possibility* that no one could have anticipated just ten years ago.

Free:

> Within ten years, we could meet 25 percent of our energy needs with solar energy, freeing ourselves of dependence on foreign oil.

(Many of these sentences should also be edited for redundancy, wordiness, heavy nominalizations, etc.)

1. Many different school systems are making a return back to old-fashioned traditional education in the *basics*. (a change)
2. Within the period of the next few years or so, automobile manufacturers will not be able to avoid meeting new and more stringent-type mileage *requirements*. (a challenge)
3. The reasons why we age are a *matter* that has puzzled and perplexed humanity for millennia. (mystery)
4. The majority of the young people in the modern world of today cannot even begin to achieve an understanding or grasp of the *insecurity* that a large number of older people had experience of during the period known as the Great Depression. (a failure)
5. The successful accomplishment of test-tube fertilization of embryos raised many *issues* of an ethical nature that continue to trouble both scientists and laypeople. (an event)
6. Many people who lived during the Victorian era were appalled when Darwin put forth the suggestion that their ancestry might have included apes.
7. In 1961 the U.S. government made the announcement that we would put the first man on the moon.
8. Nikita Khrushchev once advanced the claim that by 1975 communism would bury the system of capitalism.
9. In the 1960s the Supreme Court passed the rule that anyone under arrest for a crime that he or she might or might not have committed had to be given the widest possible benefit of legal doubt.
10. American prisons are for the most part schools for crime and pits of degradation.

In these next, prune the redundancy and the abstraction and create coordinate modifiers of your own devising. For example, here is a coordinate resumptive modifier built on to number 5 above:

> . . . ethical *issues* that are troubling both scientists and laymen, *issues* that yield easily to neither historical religious principles nor contemporary legal theory.

11. The general concept of systematic skepticism is in effect a kind of denial that there can ever be any kind of certain knowledge of reality screened and influenced by human perception.
12. The originating point when the field of scientific inquiry began to develop is to be found for the most part in the individual and personal observations of naive primitive peoples about the natural things that appear to occur in a regular way.
13. In the period known to scholars and historians as the Renaissance period, increases in affluence and stability in the area of political affairs had the practical consequence and outcome of allowing streams of thought of various different kinds to merge and flow together with one another.
14. During the recent period of about the last few years or so, we have been witness to a very large number of various specific acts and deeds that mainly involve terroristic components.

MOVEMENT AND MOMENTUM

A well-managed long sentence can be just as clear and crisp as several short ones. A writer who can handle a long sentence gracefully lets us take a breath at reasonable intervals and at appropriate places; one part of the sentence will echo another with coordinated and parallel elements. And if she avoids muddling about in abstraction and weak passives, each sentence will move with the directness and energy that a readable style demands.

But if a sentence is to flow easily, its writer should also avoid making us hesitate over words and phrases that break its major grammatical links—subject-verb, verb-object. We should be able to complete those links quickly and surely. Here, for example, is a sentence that does not flow:

> China, in order to exert in a more direct way its influence among the Eastern Bloc nations, in 1958 began in a carefully orchestrated manner a diplomatic offensive against the Soviet Union.

This flows more smoothly:

> In 1958, in order to exert a more direct influence among the Eastern Bloc nations, China began a carefully orchestrated diplomatic offensive against the Soviet Union.

Both sentences make us pause, but the first forces us to hold our breath after the subject, *China,* until we reach the verb, *began.* The second lets us take a breath halfway through, when we finish the second introductory phrase, and then quickly connect the subject with its verb. The two versions differ only in the order of the phrases. In the first sentence, the interrupting phrases break the important grammatical connections:

China > . . . . < began

in order to exert > . . . . < its influence

in a more direct way

In the second, the important grammatical connections remain intact:

. . . in order to exert > < its influence > < in a more direct way,

China > < began

And in the first, the phrases are ordered from longer to shorter; in the second, from shorter to longer. A long introductory chunk forces the reader to hold the content in mind before completing it with the second half.

Grammatical Connections

In most sentences the normal word order is subject-verb-object. If you delay or muddy the subject-verb connection, your reader may have to hesitate, backtrack, reread looking for it.

It's true that competent writers may interrupt the subject-verb link with phrases and clauses. And it's true that many short adverbs fit between subject and verb quite comfortably:

> Scientists the world over *deliberately* write in a style that is aloof, impersonal, and objective.

But longer phrases and clauses fit less comfortably:

Scientists the world over, because they deliberately write in a style that is aloof, impersonal, and objective, have difficulty communicating with laypeople.

If nothing else precedes the subject, you lose little by moving a long modifying phrase or clause to the beginning of its sentence:

Because scientists the world over deliberately write in a style that is aloof, impersonal, and objective, they have difficulty communicating with laypeople.

When you place your modifier at the beginning of its sentence, you avoid that flicker of hesitation which, if repeated, can break the flow.

Exercise 7–2

These sentences contain unfortunate interruptions. Correct the interruption and add a summative, resumptive, or free modifier of your own creation. Also edit to eliminate wordiness.

1. The construction of the Interstate Highway System, owing to the fact that Congress, on the occasion when it originally voted funds for it, did not anticipate the cost of inflation, has run into insoluble problems.
2. Such conduct or behavior, for whatever reasons proffered, is rarely not at least to some degree prejudicial to good order and discipline.
3. TV game shows, due to the fact that they have an appeal to the basic cupidity in us all, are just about the most popular shows that appear on daytime TV.
4. The merit selection of those who serve as judges, given the low quality and character of elected officials, is an idea whose time came long ago.
5. The field of high-energy physics, working with certain devices that can actually accelerate particles to a speed almost as fast as the speed of light, is exploring the ultimate nature and makeup of matter.
6. The continued and unabated emission of carbon dioxide gas into the atmospheric environment, unless there is a marked reduction prior to the end of the century, will eventually result in a change in the climate of the world as we know it today.

7. Only those individuals who are the rich, in the case that the government in advance of the next congressional election does not make any provisions for all political candidates for office to receive campaign funds, will, in large enough numbers to assure a wide selection of candidates, have the ability for seeking public office.

8. Insistence that there is no proof by scientific means of a certain causal link between the activity of smoking and various disease entities such as cardiac heart failure and malignant cancer conditions, despite the fact that there is a strong statistical correlation between the act of smoking and disease, continues to be the official stated position and policy of the cigarette companies.

9. Medical science, in about the last half century or so, due to the fact of great strides being made in the detection and even anticipation of sicknesses and diseases that in the last half century would simply make an appearance in our midst to result in the terrible devastation of whole populations, now has a year in advance the capability for the early prediction of future outbreaks of disease entities such as influenza.

Small Connections

Sometimes we awkwardly split an adjective from the modifying phrase that follows by putting the adjective before the noun it modifies, and the phrase that modifies the adjective after:

> The accountant has given *as accurate* a **projection** *as any that could be provided.*

> *We are facing a more serious* **decision** *than what you described earlier.*

> A *close* **relationship** *to the one just discovered* is the degree to which *similar* **genetic material** to that of related species can be modified by *different* **DNA chains** *from the ones first selected by Adams and Walsh.*

> *Another* **course of action** *than the present one* is necessary to accumulate *sufficient* **capital** *to complete such* **projects** *as those you have described.*

In each case, the adjective—usually an adjective being compared—is split from its following phrase:

as accurate . . . as any that could be provided
more serious . . . than what
close . . . to the one
similar . . . to that
different . . . from the ones
another . . . than the present
sufficient . . . to complete
such . . . as those you

We can maintain a smoother, unbroken rhythm if we put the adjective *after* the noun, directly next to the phrase that completes the adjective:

> The accountant has given a **projection** *as accurate as any that could have been provided.*

> We are facing a **decision** *more serious than what you described earlier.*

> A **relationship** *close to the one just discovered* is the degree to which **genetic material** *similar to that of related species* can be modified by **DNA chains** *different from the ones first selected by Adams and Walsh.*

> A **course of action** *other than the present one* is necessary to accumulate **capital** *sufficient to complete* **projects** *such as those you describe.*

Some of the adjectives that we most frequently split off from their modifying phrases are these: *more . . . than, less . . . than, other . . . than, as . . . as, similar . . . to, equal . . . to, identical . . . to, same . . . as, different . . . from, such . . . as, separate . . . from, distant . . . from, related . . . to, close . . . to, next . . . to, difficult . . . to, easy . . . to, necessary . . . to, sufficient . . . to, adequate . . . to.*

Exercise 7-3

The following sentences contain adjective phrases that have been awkwardly disjoined. Revise the passages to reunite the phrases and to make the style clearer and more direct. The separated phrases in (1) are italicized.

1. The reason why an *identical* ecological impact statement *to* that submitted the previous year indicates that it will again be *difficult*

data *to evaluate* is that there is still no *independent* verifying information *from* that which has been supplied by the applicant in our possession.

2. Under circumstances in which similar EKG readings are obtained to those obtained earlier, other conditions than cardiac insufficiency must come under suspicion. The same procedures as those outlined in the previous section must be closely adhered to on the expectation that as effective results as those outlined there are to be achieved in such cases.

3. As a result of the reorganization of the marketing research division, more accurate information than that which has been received in the past should allow the identification of different populations from those that have been traditionally aimed at. This will be relatively easy information to process in analysis as a result of the fact that there has already been accumulated such demographic data as the average financial income, expenditure patterns, etc., for many different markets. As a result of all this, greater efficiency than that which we achieved in our earlier operation last year may be a reasonable expectation.

SOME PROBLEMS WITH MODIFIERS

Sentences can grow both long and confusing when we add several modifiers, because the logical and grammatical connections between the modifier and the thing modified sometimes become unclear or ambiguous.

Dangling Modifiers

A modifier "dangles" when its implied subject differs from the specific subject of the clause that follows it:

> In order to contain the epidemic, the area was sealed off.

The implied subject of *contain,* some person or agency, is different from the subject of the main clause, *the area.*

> Resuming negotiations after a break of several days, the same issues confronted both the union and the company.

The implied subject of *resuming, the union and the company,* is different from the subject of the main clause, *the same issues.*

Constructions like these more often amuse than confuse us. But since they cause some readers to hesitate for a moment, you ought to avoid them on general principles. Either rewrite the introductory phrase so that it has its own subject or make the subject of the main clause agree with the implied subject of the introductory phrase:

> In order for *us* to contain the epidemic, the area was sealed off.
> In order to contain the epidemic, the *city* sealed off the area.

> When *the union and the company* resumed negotiations, the same issues confronted them.
> Resuming negotiations after a break of several days, *the union and the company* confronted the same issues.

Some modifiers that seem to dangle are in fact acceptable. If either the modifier or the subject of the main clause is part of the metadiscourse, the modifier will seem entirely appropriate to most readers:

> *In order to start the motor,* **it is essential** that the retroflex cam connecting rod be disengaged.

> **To summarize,** *unemployment* in the southern tier of counties remains the state's major economic and social problem.

Misplaced Modifiers

A second problem with modifiers is that sometimes they seem to modify two things, or the wrong thing. One kind of ambiguous modifier can refer either forward or back:

> Overextending oneself in strenuous physical activity *too frequently* results in a variety of physical ailments.

> We failed *entirely* to understand the complexities of the problem.

In each of these, the modifier can just as easily appear in an unambiguous position:

> Overextending oneself *too frequently* in strenuous exercise. . . .

> Overextending oneself in physical exercise results *too frequently* in a variety of physical ailments.

> We *entirely* failed to understand. . . .
> We failed to understand *entirely*. . . .

A second ambiguity occurs when a modifier at the end of a clause or sentence can modify either a neighboring or a more distant phrase:

> Scientists have learned that their observations are as necessarily subjective as those in any other field *in recent years.*

We can move the modifier to a less ambiguous position:

> *In recent years,* scientists have learned that. . . .
> Scientists have learned that *in recent years,* their observations. . . .

In these cases, we can also use a resumptive modifier to clarify what a modifier is supposed to modify. In the next sentence, for example, what is it that dictates—the relationships, the components, or the process?

> Perhaps there are relationships among the components of the process that would dictate one order rather than another.

A moment's thought suggests that the relationships dictate, but why should we cause our reader to pause even for a moment to understand how one idea connects to another? A resumptive modifier would make it clear:

> Perhaps there are relationships among the components of the process, *relationships* that would dictate one order rather than another.

Pronoun Reference

A long sentence can also create problems with pronoun reference. If there is the slightest chance that a pronoun will confuse your reader, don't hesitate to repeat the antecedent. And if you can conveniently make one of your nouns plural and another singular, you can use singular and plural pronouns to distinguish what you're referring to.
Compare these:

> *Physicians* must never forget that *their patients* are vitally concerned about *their* treatment and *their* prognosis, but that *they* are often unwilling to ask for fear of what *they* will say.

A physician must never forget that *his patients* are vitally concerned about *their* treatment and *their* prognosis, but that *they* are often unwilling to ask for fear of what *he* will say.

(We'll take up the matter of the masculine *he* in Lesson Ten.)

Exercise 7–4

Rearrange the elements in these sentences so that they flow more easily.

1. The heightened sense of responsibility as a nation in recent years toward improving the pre-school educational preparation of disadvantaged children has led to these higher achievement scores in early grades, according to many other reports, however.
2. I will now sketch the solar system as it was conceived by pre-Copernican astronomers ordinarily in simple outline for you.
3. Historians impose not just their private view of historical relevancy but the implied view of their whole social matrix on the past with little sense of scholarly bias.
4. We can perhaps if we study the psychoanalytic theories that Freud created for his scholarly and therefore largely male audience honestly and objectively in all their masculine assumptions understand why psychiatry has assigned the major source of a man's mental disorder to his mother so often.
5. The isolation of various clotting mechanisms in higher mammals is the next point.
6. The relation of individual objective bits of data to general principles applicable at all times and everywhere is a more important defining feature of the modern mind.
7. That Woodrow Wilson's refusal to take the leadership of the United States Senate into his confidence caused the defeat of the Versailles Treaty is universally acknowledged.
8. Two historically antagonistic chambers, a variety of hereditary and appointed senators whose responsibility in administrative affairs is relatively slight making up one and an elective body that carries on the important legislative activities making up the other, constitute the legislative branch.
9. A virus which bears no known relation to any other form of protein-based life was discovered last year, though, in England.

10. That the need to monitor the flow of hard currency across national boundaries more carefully in the years to come is an equally pressing matter is just as important, in the opinion of most international monetary experts.

These sentences suffer from a variety of dangling, misplaced, ambiguous, and otherwise badly positioned modifiers. Correct them, and then edit the sentences in any other way you see fit.

11. Having no previous familiarity with the mechanism, metal deposit detection efforts by means of its use were met with a lack of positive results.

12. With every expectation of success, new efforts to resolve the differences that have resulted in interference with communication in a short time should be initiated.

13. Realizing that the undergraduate curriculum must be completely reevaluated in the next few weeks, proposals have suddenly appeared on the agenda that had received earlier discussion.

14. After making an audit of all internal operations in the summer of 1978 a second audit examined the record of foreign affiliates that had not been previously audited by their local headquarters.

All of these devices will help you give shape to a long sentence, but if the **content** of that long sentence is incoherent, no well-formed syntax can save it. The sentence below appeared in an article in *The New York Times* travel section. It is syntactically well-formed: Its writer opens with a coherent main clause, continues with a coherent loose modifier, and concludes with a coherently coordinated pair of clauses. But deliberate or not, the progression of ideas is at best goofy. (In the preceding sentence, the writer had introduced the professional women of Amsterdam's red-light district.)

> They are so unself-conscious about their profession that by day they can be seen standing naked in doorways, chatting with their neighbors in the shadow of the Oudekerstoren Church, which offers Saturday carillon concerts at 4 P.M. and a panoramic view of the city from its tower in summer.

Clarity and grace without a controlling idea will give you only the outside of a well-turned sentence. The inside provides the substance that supports the external design.

SUMMING UP
Managing Long Sentences

1. Avoid writing long, rhythmically unbroken sentences consisting of one clause tacked on to another tacked on to another tacked on to another. Instead, use one or more of the following devices:

    a. Coordination

    Besides the fact that no previous civilization has experienced such rapid alterations in the condition of daily life, the life of the mind has changed greatly too.

    No previous civilization has experienced such rapid alterations *in the condition of daily life* or *in the life of the mind.*

    b. Resumptive modifiers

    Our discovery that the earth was not at the center of the universe reshaped our understanding not only of where we are but of who we are, which was changed again by Darwin, and again by Freud, and again by Einstein.

    Our discovery that the earth was not at the center of the universe reshaped *our understanding* not only of where we are but of who we are, *an understanding* that was changed again by Darwin, and again by Freud, and again by Einstein.

    c. Summative modifiers

    Most business people and government officials have maintained that the only way to anticipate future energy crises is to construct a massive synthetic fuel industry, which is rejected by those environmentalists who argue that we can achieve the same net result by equally massive investments in mass transportation and insulation.

    Most business people and government officials have maintained that the only way to anticipate future energy crises is to construct a massive synthetic fuel industry, *a position* rejected by those environmentalists who argue that we can achieve the same net result by equally massive investments in mass transportation and insulation.

d. Free modifiers

The Dog Whelk is one of the most common snails found in the intertidal zone of the northern East Coast which proliferates in especially dense colonies on rocky shelves from Maine all the way to the Arctic Circle.

The Dog Whelk is one of the most common snails found in the intertidal zone of the northern East Coast, *proliferating* in especially dense colonies on rocky shelves from Maine all the way to the Arctic Circle.

2. To keep up the momentum in a long sentence, don't break the links between subject and verb or verb and object:

The Protagoras, *despite its questionable logic and rather superficial philosophical content,* **remains** one of Plato's most dramatically appealing dialogues.

Despite its questionable logic and rather superficial philosophical content, **the Protagoras remains** one of Plato's most dramatically appealing dialogues.

On the other hand, if the object is very long and the interrupting phrase is very short, put the modifier between the verb and object.

Few politicians are willing to acknowledge that the bulk of the electorate regards them essentially as parasites *even to themselves.*

Few politicians are willing to acknowledge *even to themselves* that the bulk of the electorate regards them essentially as parasites.

3. Watch for and revise modifiers that do not seem to modify what you intend them to:

Re-examining the issues that had been earlier discussed, a new perspective on them arose among the committee.

Re-examining the issues that it had earlier discussed, the committee developed a new perspective on them.

International terrorism is a problem for which our system of government had no good solution, because in order to deal with it terrorists have to be the objects of sudden and unexpected preemptive attacks directed at targets located in other countries that must be obliterated quickly and without public debate.

International terrorism is a problem for which our system of government has no good solution. In order to deal with foreign-based terrorists, we have to direct sudden and pre-emptive attacks at *targets* located in other countries, *targets* that must be obliterated quickly and without public debate.

A Touch of Class

Anything is better than not to write clearly. There is nothing to be said against lucidity, and against simplicity only the possibility of dryness. This is a risk well worth taking when you reflect how much better it is to be bald than to wear a curly wig.

SOMERSET MAUGHAM

But clarity and brevity, though a good beginning, are only a beginning. By themselves, they may remain bare and bleak. When Calvin Coolidge, asked by his wife what the preacher had preached on, replied "Sin," and, asked what the preacher had said, replied "He was against it," he was brief enough. But one hardly envies Mrs. Coolidge.

F. L. LUCAS

There are two sorts of eloquence; the one indeed scarce deserves the name of it, which consists chiefly in laboured and polished periods, an over-curious and artificial arrangement of figures, tinselled over with a gaudy embellishment of words, ... The other sort of eloquence is quite the reverse to this, and which may be said to be the true characteristic of the holy Scriptures; where the eloquence does not arise from a laboured and far-fetched elocution, but from a surprising mixture of simplicity and majesty, ...

LAURENCE STERNE

Let's assume that you can now write clear, cohesive, and appropriately emphatic prose. That in itself would constitute a style of such singular distinction that most of us would be satisfied to have achieved so much. But even though we might prefer bald clarity to the turgidity of most institutional prose, the relentless simplicity of the plain style can finally become flat and dry, eventually arid. Its plainness invests prose with the blandness of unsalted meat and potatoes—honest fare to be sure, but hardly memorable and certainly without zest. Sometimes a touch of class, a flash of elegance, can mark the difference between forgettable Spartan prose and an idea so elegantly expressed that it fixes itself in the mind of your reader.

Now, I can't tell you how to be graceful and elegant in the same way I can tell you how to be clear and direct. What I *can* do is describe some of the devices that some graceful writers use. But that advice is, finally, about as useful as listing the ingredients in the bouillabaisse of a great cook and then expecting anyone to make it. Knowing the ingredients and knowing how to use them is the difference between reading cookbooks and Cooking.

What follows describes a few ingredients of a modestly elegant style. How imaginatively and skillfully you use them is the difference between reading this book on writing, and Writing.

BALANCE AND SYMMETRY

We've already described how you can use coordination to extend a sentence beyond a few words (pp. 127–30). Coordination itself will grace a sentence with a movement more rhythmic and satisfying than that of a noncoordinate sentence or sentences. Compare these two versions of Walter Lippmann's argument about the need for a balance of powers in a democratic society.

> The national unity of a free people depends upon a sufficiently even balance of political power to make it impracticable for the administration to be arbitrary and for the opposition to be revolutionary and irreconcilable. Where that balance no longer exists, democracy perishes. For unless all the citizens of a state are forced by circumstances to compromise, unless they feel that they can affect policy but that no one can wholly dominate it, unless by habit and necessity they have to give and take, freedom cannot be maintained.

The national unity of a free people depends upon a sufficiently
even balance of political power to make it impracticable for there
to be an arbitrary administration against a revolutionary opposition
that is irreconcilably opposed to it. Where that balance no longer
exists, democracy perishes. For unless all the citizens of a state are
habitually forced by necessary circumstances to compromise in a
way that lets them affect policy with no one dominating it, freedom
cannot be maintained.

In my version, the sentences just run on from one phrase to the next,
from one clause to another. In his version, Lippmann balances phrase
against phrase, clause against clause, creating an almost architectural
symmetry through the whole passage. We can see more clearly how his
sentences work if we break them out into their parts.

The national unity of a free people depends upon a sufficiently even
balance of political power to make it impracticable

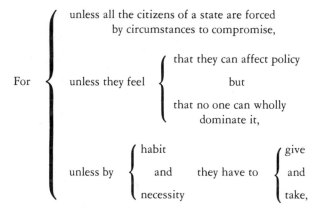

Where that balance no longer exists, democracy perishes.

freedom cannot be maintained.

We can enhance the rhythm and grace of coordination if we keep in mind a few simple principles. First, a coordinate series will move more gracefully if each succeeding coordinate element is longer than the one before it. So if you coordinate within a coordination, do it in the last element.

We can use correlative conjunctions such as *both X and Y, not only X but also Y, neither X nor Y* to signify a balanced coordination and to give it emphasis.

Compare these:

The national significance of an ethnic minority depends upon a sufficiently deep historical identity that makes it

{ impossible that the majority will absorb the minority

and

inevitable that the minority will { maintain its identity

and

transmit its heritage.

The national significance of an ethnic minority depends upon a sufficiently deep historical identity that makes it

{ **not only** impossible that the majority will absorb the minority

but

inevitable that the minority will { **both** maintain its identity

and

transmit its heritage.

The second is clearly stronger than the first.

You can make these coordinate patterns more rhetorically elegant if you consciously balance parts of phrases and clauses against one another:

Neither { the vacuous emotion of daytime soap opera

nor

the mindless eroticism of nighttime sitcoms

reflects the best { *that American artists are able to create*

or

that American audiences are willing to support.

The richest kind of balance and parallelism counterpoints both grammar and meaning: here *vacuous* is balanced against *mindless, emotion* against *eroticism, daytime* against *nighttime, soap opera* against *sitcoms, artists* against *audiences, able* against *willing,* and *create* against *support.*

You can achieve the same effect when you balance parts of sentences that are *not* coordinated. Here is a subject balanced against an object. The square brackets signal a balanced but not *coordinate* pair.

Scientists who tear down established views of the universe
               invariably challenge
those of us who have built up our visions of reality upon
               those views.

Here, the predicate of a relative clause in a subject is balanced against the predicate of that subject:

A government that is unwilling to
  listen to the moderate voices of its citizenry
  must eventually answer to the harsh justice of its revolutionaries.

A direct object balanced against the object of a preposition:

Those of us who are vitally concerned about our failing school systems are not quite ready to sacrifice
  the intellectual growth of our innocent children
                  to
  the social daydreaming of irresponsible bureaucrats.

Here is a main clause balanced against a subordinate clause and then a direct object and two prepositional objects balanced against one another:

Were [*I trading*   [*my scholarly principles*
                        for
                financial security,

      I would scarcely be writing   [*short books*
                                           on
                                     minor subjects
                                          for
                                     small audiences.

None of these are coordinated, but they are all consciously balanced. Like every other artful device, these balanced phrases and clauses can eventually become self-defeating—or at least monotonously arch. But if you use them unobtrusively when you want to emphasize an important point or conclude the line of an argument, you can give your prose a shape and a cadence that most ordinary writing lacks.

Exercise 8-1

Pick five or six sentences that have been laid out schematically in this lesson or in any of the previous lessons and imitate their structural patterns. Don't try to imitate the sentences word for word or even phrase for phrase. Simply try to follow the general structural pattern of the example. For example, here's a sentence with a second coordination in the object:

A contemplative life in the country

{ requires the energy to overcome the brute facts of an uncooperative Nature

but

rewards the person who has that energy
{ with the unmatchable satisfaction of having done it

and

with an inner confidence that makes contemplation meaningful.

First, think of a subject close enough to this one to make your imitation easy—for example, the academic life:

Life as a college professor
{ offers summer vacations longer than most

but

imposes a sense of guilt on that person who
{ ignores his or her scholarly work

and

enjoys the time the profession offers.

Try laying out your sentence in the way the model is schematically arranged, but then write it out in the usual way, so that you can get the feel of a long sentence as it unfolds before you.

Some of the sentences you might imitate are on pages 127–30, 150–52.

Here are the first halves of some balanced sentences. Finish them with last halves that balance the first halves.

1. Those who keep silent over the loss of small freedoms . . .
2. While the strong are never afraid to admit their real weaknesses, the weak . . .
3. We should pay more attention to those politicians who tell us how to make what we have better than to those . . .
4. When parents raise children who do not value the importance of hard work, the adults those children become . . .
5. Too many teachers mistake neat papers rehashing conventional ideas for . . .

In these next exercises, you must invent material to fit the patterns. Use other verbs, if they allow you to follow the pattern.

6. trade X for Y (for example: I would never *trade* an immediate but transitory pleasure *for* a distant but enduring virtue.)
7. mistake X for Y
8. substitute X for Y
9. balance X against Y
10. sell X for Y

EMPHASIS AND RHYTHM

As we have seen, emphasis is largely a matter of controlling the way a sentence ends. When we maneuver our most important information into that stressed position, the natural emphasis we hear in our mind's ear underscores the rhetorical emphasis of a significant idea. But the sentence will still seem weak and anticlimactic if it ends with lightweight words.

Different parts of speech carry different weights. Prepositions are very light—one reason why we sometimes avoid leaving a preposition at the end. Sentences should move toward strength; a preposition can dilute that strength.

Compare:

The intellectual differences among races is a subject that only the most politically indifferent scientist *is willing to look into.*

The intellectual differences among races is a subject that only the most politically indifferent scientist *is willing to explore.*

Adjectives and adverbs are heavier than prepositions, but lighter than verbs and nouns. The heaviest, the most emphatic words are nominalizations, those abstract nouns that in Lesson Two we worked so hard to eliminate. But we worked hard to eliminate them mostly at the beginnings of sentences, where you want to get off to a brisk start. When you end a sentence with a nominalization, you create a different effect. You bring the sentence to an end with a climactic thump.

Compare these two versions of Winston Churchill's "Finest Hour" speech, in which Churchill, always the elegant and emphatic writer, ends with the elegant parallelism emphasized by the pair of nominalizations:

> . . . until in God's good time, the New World, with all its power and might, steps forth to the **rescue** and the **liberation** of the old.

He could have written more simply, more directly, and much more banally:

> . . . until in God's good time, the powerful New World steps forth to liberate the old.

In this next passage, E.B. White was writing about a rather less dramatic event, the death of a favorite pig. But White wanted to elevate the scene to one approaching tragedy, so he drew on the same stylistic resources that Churchill used:

I have written this account
{
  {
    in **penitence**
      and
    in **grief**
      as a man who failed to raise his pig

    and

    to explain my **deviation** from the
      classic course of so many raised pigs.
  }
}

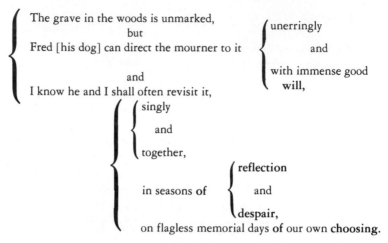

The grave in the woods is unmarked,
        but
Fred [his dog] can direct the mourner to it

        and
I know he and I shall often revisit it,

        singly

        and

        together,

    in seasons of   reflection
                      and
                      despair,

    on flagless memorial days of our own **choosing.**

        unerringly
          and
    with immense good
        will,

He could have written

> As a man who failed to raise his pig, I have grieved as I have written this account in order to explain why I deviated from the classic course of so many raised pigs. Although the grave in the woods is unmarked, Fred can unerringly direct the mourner to it with good will. I know the two of us shall often revisit it, at those times when we are reflecting on things and when we are despairing, on flagless memorial days that we shall choose.

But without the elegant touches, without the parallelisms and the emphatic final nominalizations, the passage becomes merely silly.

Here is a passage by the political scientist and statesman, George Kennan, in which he describes Averell Harriman, ambassador to the Soviet Union during World War II, a man of great dedication and elegance. Which of these passages better reflects Harriman's style is obvious:

> He had that curious contempt for elegance that only the wealthy can normally afford . . . in Moscow, [his] interest was, properly and commendably, the prospering of the American war effort and American diplomacy as President Roosevelt viewed and understood it. To the accomplishment of his part in the furtherance of this objective he addressed himself with a dedication, a persistence, and an unflagging energy and attention that has no parallel in my experience. . . . His physical frame, spare and sometimes ailing, seemed at best an unwelcome irrelevance. I had the impression that it was with an angry impatience that he took cognizance of the

occasional reminders of its existence, dragged it with him on his daily rounds of duty, and forced it to support him where continuation without its support was not possible.

He had that curious contempt for elegant things that only wealthy people can normally afford . . . in Moscow, he was interested, properly and commendably, only in helping the American war effort and American diplomatic affairs as President Roosevelt viewed and understood them. To accomplish his part in this objective he addressed himself in a dedicated and persistent way, with an unflagging energy and attention that parallels nothing I have experienced. . . . His physical frame, spare and sometimes ailing, seemed at best unwelcome and irrelevant. It seemed to me that he was angry and impatient when he recognized those times when it reminded him that it existed, dragged it with him on his daily rounds of duty, and forced it to support him where he could not have continued without it.

Now, when a writer combines nominalizations with balanced and parallel constructions, when he draws on resumptive and summative modifiers to extend the line of a sentence, we know he is cranking up a style that aims at elegant complexity. This sentence by Frederick Jackson Turner, from his *The Frontier in American History,* displays most of those devices, plus one more. If you seek an *extravagantly* elegant style, construct elaborately balanced units, sprinkle them with nominalizations, and then—this will sound odd—end clauses with phrases introduced by *of:* "This is the heritage **of pioneer experience**—."

> This then is the heritage of pioneer experience—a passionate belief that a democracy was possible which should leave the individual a part to play in free society and not make him a cog in a machine operated from above; which trusted in the common man, in his tolerance, his ability to adjust differences with good humor, and to work out an American type from the contributions of all nations— a type for which he would fight against those who challenged it in arms, and for which in time of war he would make sacrifices, even the temporary sacrifice of individual freedom and his life, lest that freedom be lost forever.

> This then is the heritage **of pioneer experience,**—
> (free modifier)
>   a passionate belief that a democracy was possible

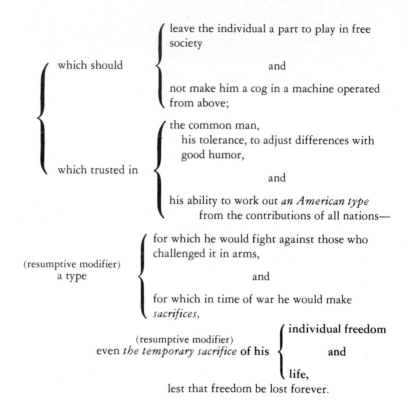

which should

leave the individual a part to play in free society

and

not make him a cog in a machine operated from above;

which trusted in

the common man,
    his tolerance, to adjust differences with
    good humor,

and

his ability to work out *an American type*
    from the contributions of all nations—

(resumptive modifier)
a type

for which he would fight against those who challenged it in arms,

and

for which in time of war he would make *sacrifices,*

(resumptive modifier)
even *the temporary sacrifice* of his

individual freedom

and

life,

lest that freedom be lost forever.

Exercise 8-2

In addition to other faults, these sentences end on weak adjectives and adverbs or clumsy possessives. Besides editing them for clarity and concision, revise them so that they end on more heavily stressed words, particularly on prepositional phrases beginning with *of*. For example:

> Our interest in ESP, UFOs, and other paranormal phenomena testifies to the fact that we have empty spirits and shallow minds.

> Our interest in ESP, UFOs, and other paranormal phenomena testifies to the emptiness of our spirits and the shallowness of our minds.

1. Not very many tendencies in our governmental system have brought about more changes in American daily life than federal governmental agencies that are very powerful.

2. In the year 1923 several of the representatives from the side of the

victorious Allied nations went to Versailles with the intention of seeking to dismember Germany's economic potential and to destroy her armaments industry.

3.   The day is eliminated when school systems' boards of education have the expectation that local area taxpayers will automatically go along with whatever extravagant things administrators decide to do.

4.   The blueprint for the political campaign plan was concocted by the mayor's advisers who are least sensitive.

5.   If we invest our sweat in these projects, we must avoid appearing to be working only because we are interested in ourselves.

6.   Irreplaceable works of native art are progressing into slow deterioration in many of our most prestigious museums for the reason that their curators have no recognition of how extremely fragile even recent artifacts can be.

7.   Throughout history, science has made progress because dedicated scientists have gotten around a hostile public that is uninformed.

LENGTH AND RHYTHM

In ordinary prose, the length of your sentences becomes an issue only if they are all about fifteen words long or if they are all much longer, over thirty or so. Though one eighteen-to-twenty-word sentence after another isn't the ideal goal, they will seem less monotonous than a series of sentences that are regularly and significantly longer or shorter.

In artful prose, on the other hand, length is more deliberately controlled. Some accomplished stylists can write one short sentence after another, perhaps to strike a note of urgency:

> Toward noon Petrograd again became the field of military action; rifles and machine guns rang out everywhere. It was not easy to tell who was shooting or where. One thing was clear; the past and the future were exchanging shots. There was much casual firing; young boys were shooting off revolvers unexpectedly acquired. The arsenal was wrecked. . . . Shots rang out on both sides. But the board fence stood in the way, dividing the soldiers from the revolution. The attackers decided to break down the fence. They broke down part of it and set fire to the rest. About twenty barracks came into view. The bicyclists were concentrated in two or three of them. The empty barracks were set fire to at once.
>
> —Leon Trotsky, *The Russian Revolution* trans. by Max Eastman

Or terse certainty:

> The teacher or lecturer is a danger. He very seldom recognizes his nature or his position. The lecturer is a man who must talk for an hour. France may possibly have acquired the intellectual leadership of Europe when their academic period was cut down to forty minutes. I also have lectured. The lecturer's first problem is to have enough words to fill forty or sixty minutes. The professor is paid for his time, his results are almost impossible to estimate. . . . No teacher has ever failed from ignorance. That is empiric professional knowledge. Teachers fail because they cannot "handle the class." Real education must ultimately be limited to men who INSIST on knowing, the rest is mere sheep-herding.
>
> —Ezra Pound, *ABC of Reading*

Or fire:

> Let us look at this American artist first. How did he ever get to America, to start with? Why isn't he a European still, like his father before him?
>
> Now listen to me, don't listen to him. He'll tell you the lie you expect. Which is partly your fault for expecting it.
>
> He didn't come in search of freedom of worship. England had more freedom of worship in the year 1700 than America had. Won by Englishmen who wanted freedom and so stopped at home and fought for it. And got it. Freedom of worship? Read the history of New England during the first century of its existence.
>
> Freedom anyhow? The land of the free! This the land of the free! Why, if I say anything that displeases them, the free mob will lynch me, and that's my freedom. Free? Why I have never been in any country where the individual has such an abject fear of his fellow countrymen. Because, as I say, they are free to lynch him the moment he shows he is not one of them. . . .
>
> All right then, what did they come for? For lots of reasons. Perhaps least of all in search of freedom of any sort: positive freedom, that is.
>
> —D.H. Lawrence, *Studies in Classic American Literature*

In this last example, Lawrence invests his discourse with even more urgency by breaking sentences into fragments and what could be longer paragraphs into abrupt snatches of discourse.

Equally accomplished writers write one long sentence after another to suggest a mind exploring an idea in the act of writing the sentence:

In any event, up at the front of this March, in the first line, back of
that hollow square of monitors, Mailer and Lowell walked in this
barrage of cameras, helicopters, TV cars, monitors, loudspeakers,
and wavering buckling twisting line of notables, arms linked (line
twisting so much that at times the movement was in file, one arm
locked ahead, one behind, then the line would undulate about and
the other arm would be ahead) speeding up a few steps, slowing
down while a great happiness came back into the day as if finally
one stood under some mythical arch in the great vault of history,
helicopters buzzing about, chop-chop, and the sense of America
divided on this day now liberated some undiscovered patriotism in
Mailer so that he felt a sharp searing love for his country in this
moment and on this day, crossing some divide in his own mind
wider than the Potomac, a love so lacerated he felt as if a marriage
were being torn and children lost—never does one love so much as
then, obviously, then—and an odor of wood smoke, from where
you knew not, was also in the air, a smoke of dignity and some
calm heroism, not unlike the sense of freedom which also comes
when a marriage is burst—Mailer knew for the first time why men
in the front line of battle are almost always ready to die; there is a
promise of some swift transit. . . .

—Norman Mailer, *Armies of the Night*

This single punctuated sentence goes on for several hundred more words.

Exercise 8-3

First, imitate a passage that has a series of very short sentences. Then
imitate the Mailer sentence (you might want to read the rest of it in Book I,
Part III, Chapter 4, of *Armies of the Night*). Then try to revise the passages
made up of short sentences into just one or two long sentences, each in the
style of Mailer. Then revise the Mailer passage into a series of short, curt
sentences.

METAPHOR

Clarity, vigor, symmetry, rhythm—prose so graced would more than
satisfy most of us. And yet, if it offered no virtues other than these, such
prose would excite an admiration only for our craft, not for the reach of our
imagination. This next passage displays all the stylistic graces we've

described, but it goes beyond mere craft. It reveals a truth about pleasure through a figure of speech embedded in a comparison that is itself almost metaphorical.

> The secret of the enjoyment of pleasure is to know when to stop.
> . . . We do this every time we listen to music. We do not seize hold
> of a particular chord or phrase and shout at the orchestra to go on
> playing it for the rest of the evening; on the contrary, however
> much we may like that particular moment of music, we know that
> its perpetuation would interrupt and kill the movement of the
> melody. We understand that the beauty of a symphony is less in
> these musical moments than in the whole movement from begin-
> ning to end. If the symphony tries to go on too long, if at a certain
> point the composer exhausts his creative ability and tries to carry
> on just for the sake of filling in the required space of time, then we
> begin to fidget in our chairs, feeling that he has denied the natural
> rhythm, has broken the smooth curve from birth to death, and that
> though a pretense of life is being made, it is in fact a living death.
>
> —Alan W. Watts, *The Meaning of Happiness*

Watts could have written this:

> . . . however much we may like that particular moment of music,
> we know that its perpetuation would interrupt and spoil the
> movement of the melody. . . . we begin to fidget in our chairs,
> feeling that he has denied the natural rhythm, has interrupted the
> regular movement from beginning to end, and that though a pre-
> tense of wholeness is being made, it is in fact a repeated end.

The two passages are equally clear and graceful. But the first illumi-
nates music—and pleasure—in a way the second does not. The metaphor
of birth and the smooth, unbroken curve of life into death startles us with a
flash of unexpected truth.

Of metaphor, Aristotle wrote,

> By far the greatest thing is to be a master of metaphor. It is the
> one thing that cannot be learned from others. It is a sign of genius,
> for a good metaphor implies an intuitive perception of similarity
> among dissimilars.

A metaphor invites us to look at a familiar thing in a new way. Similes do
the same, but less intensely, the *like* or *as* moderating the force of the
comparison.

Compare these:

> The schoolmaster is the person who takes the children off the parents' hands for a consideration. That is to say, he establishes a child prison, engages a number of employee schoolmasters as turn-keys, and covers up the essential cruelty and unnaturalness of the situation by torturing the children if they do not learn, and calling this process, which is within the capacity of any fool or blackguard, by the sacred name of Teaching.
>
> —G. B. Shaw, *Sham Education*

> . . . he establishes something like a child prison, engages a number of employee schoolmasters to act like turnkeys, covers up the essential cruelty and unnaturalness of the situation by doing things to the children that are like torture if they do not learn. . . . calling this process, which is within the capacity of any fool or blackguard, by the sacred name of Teaching.

Both passages say the same thing about education, but the first with more intensity and immediacy.

You may think that metaphor is appropriate only to poetic writing, or reflective or polemical writing. But metaphor vivifies all kinds of prose. Many historians rely on it:

> This is what may be called the common-sense view of history. History consists of a corpus of ascertained facts. The facts are available to the historian in documents, inscriptions, and so on, like fish on the fishmonger's slab. The historian collects them, takes them home, and cooks and serves them in whatever style appeals to him. Acton, whose culinary tastes were austere, wanted them served plain. . . . Sir George Clark, critical as he was of Acton's attitude, himself contrasts the "hard core of facts" in history with the "surrounding pulp of disputable interpretation"—forgetting perhaps that the pulpy part of the fruit is more rewarding than the hard core.
>
> —E. H. Carr, *What Is History?*

So do biologists:

> Some of you may have been thinking that, instead of delivering a scientific address, I have been indulging in a flight of fancy. It is a flight, but not of mere fancy, nor is it just an individual indulgence. It is my small personal attempt to share in the flight of the mind into new realms of our cosmic environment. We have evolved

> wings for such flights, in the shape of the disciplined scientific
> imagination. Support for those wings is provided by the atmo-
> sphere of knowledge created by human science and learning: so far
> as this supporting atmosphere extends, so far can our wings take us
> in our exploration.
>
> —Julian Huxley, "New Bottles for Old Wine," *Journal of the Royal
> Anthropological Institute*

And philosophers:

> Suppose I look at the night sky through a piece of heavily smoked
> glass on which certain lines have been left clear. Then I shall see
> only the stars that can be made to lie on the lines previously pre-
> pared upon the screen, and the stars I do see will be seen as
> organized by the screen's structure. We can think of a metaphor as
> such a screen. We can say that the principal subject is "seen
> through" the metaphorical expression—or, if we prefer, that the
> principal subject is "projected upon" the field of the subsidiary
> subject.
>
> —Max Black, "Metaphor," *Models and Metaphors*

And when they are writing of new ideas for which there is yet no standard language, so do physicists:

> Whereas the lepton pair has a positive rest mass when it is
> regarded as a single particle moving with a velocity equal to the
> vector sum of the motions of its two components, a photon always
> has zero rest mass. This difference can be glossed over, however, by
> treating the lepton pair as the offspring of the decay of a short-
> lived photonlike parent called a virtual photon.
>
> —Leon M. Lederman, "The Upsilon Particle," *Scientific American*

These metaphors serve different ends. Shaw used the prison metaphor to emphasize a point that he could have made without it. But prisons,
turnkeys, and torture invest his argument with an emotional intensity that
ordinary language could not communicate. Carr used fish and fruit both to
emphasize and to illuminate. He could have expressed his ideas more
prosaically, but the literal statement would have been longer and weaker.
Black and Lederman used their comparisons not to emphasize but entirely
to explain; neither required any dramatically heightened emphasis.

But if metaphor can sometimes evidence a fresh imagination, it can
also betray those of us whose imaginations fall short of its demands. Too
often, we use metaphor to gloss over inexact thinking:

> Societies give birth to new values through the differential osmotic
> flow of daily social interaction. Conflicts evolve when new values
> collide with the old, a process that frequently spawns yet a new set
> of values that synthesize the conflict into a reconciliation of
> opposites.

We get the picture, but through a cracked glass of careless metaphor. The birth metaphor suggests a traumatic event, but the new values, it is claimed, result from osmotic flow, a process constituted by a multitude of invisibly small events. Conflicts do not usually "evolve"; they more often occur in an instant, as suggested by the metaphor of collision. The spawning image picks up the metaphor of birth again, but by this time the image is, at best, collectively ludicrous.

Had the writer thought through his ideas carefully, he might have expressed them in clearer, nonfigurative language:

> As we continuously interact with one another in small ways, we
> gradually create new social values. When one person behaves
> according to one of these new values and another according to an
> old value, the values may come into conflict, creating a new third
> value that reconciles the other two.

Less misleading, but more embarrassing, are those passages that confuse emphasis with extravagance. Huxley's passage about the wings of inquiry flapping in an atmosphere of scientific knowledge comes perilously close. This next topples into bathos:

> The slavering maw of inflation is wolfing down the hard-earned
> savings of retired people. As they plummet headlong into the pit of
> penury, they see before them only the prospect of economic
> perdition.

Metaphors also invite trouble if we aren't sensitive to their earlier literal incarnations. Many words that we use altogether prosaically originated in dead metaphors that spring back to life when we least expect it. We "look over" a problem in order to "handle" it correctly. Once we "grasp" its difficulty, we can "break" the problem down into its parts. None of these metaphors is remarkable; indeed, we are not even conscious of their being metaphors. But when we conjoin dead metaphors carelessly, we can unwittingly—and often ludicrously—resurrect their earlier meanings.

> Unless marketing research can get a feel for the tastes of the younger buyer, the thrust of any advertising campaign will be fruitless.

We can get an idea about tastes, or a feel for preferences; the thrust of a campaign may be in the wrong direction; and an effort may be fruitless. But a "feel" for a "taste" is as tasteless as a "fruitless thrust."

Sad to say, there are no simple rules for distinguishing good metaphors from bad. About the only safe rule is this: If you create a metaphor that makes you feel good every time you read it, cut it out. It's sure to be too clever by half. And if you discover yourself chasing a metaphor through more than two lines, as Huxley did, start over.

It's tempting to advise novice writers never to use metaphors: we can write clearly, persuasively, even movingly without them. But those who seek a prose style that is more than merely clear and concise might keep in mind what Dr. Johnson said of Jonathan Swift: "The rogue never hazards a metaphor." Swift was one of the great prose craftsmen of English literature, and in fact he ventured more than a few metaphors. But Johnson was right, too: For all his stylistic wit, Swift's prose lacked that flash of imagery and metaphor that makes memorable the prose of some others who could not construct a sentence half so well.

As with a sense of elegance and grace, developing a good ear—or eye—for metaphor takes practice. And perhaps Aristotle was right, too: Perhaps it cannot be learned at all. But the rewards of metaphor go beyond a style that is merely a bit more mannered than usual. Metaphor is a way of exploring a subject, a way of seeing a subject through a prism of new perspectives.

Writers beginning to experiment with metaphor will fail more often than they will succeed. Almost invariably, whenever we learn a new skill, we exercise its virtues to excess: When we first learn to drive, we steer too much; after a course in logic, we attempt to construct every argument out of rigorous syllogisms. And in matters of style, those who master a new device, a new turn of phrase, will use it everywhere. Unfortunately, failed first attempts at metaphoric flair are more embarrassing than exaggerated efforts toward clarity and simplicity. And so those entirely natural, entirely predictable early failures can embarrass and discourage even the most diligent students of style. I can only reassure those who are chagrined by their early infelicities that everyone experiences the same failures, that no one has ever easily achieved elegant simplicity, much less effortless elegance.

Exercise 8-4

The following sentences exhibit excessive length, pervasive wordiness, and some unfortunate metaphors. Edit them in whatever ways you think appropriate.

1. I would like to state that the various figures that are contained in the first quarter report that in effect seem to spell out particular numbers of importance in regard to the facts regarding productivity, particularly the hidden and unseen costs that are clearly a reflection of as yet unseen renewed pressures of an inflationary origin that are throwing a monkey wrench into our research budget, reveal the considerable degree to which we are in special need of research efforts and activities into new and innovative approaches to a way out of the skyrocketing spiral of wages and compensation for labor that is usually classed as unskilled.

2. In order that a solid grasp of the abstract heart of Einstein's theory of relativity be mastered, there is the initial necessity as to seeing the speed of light as a constant factor, regardless of and independent of where the observer rests or what the particular speed of any given observer might perhaps be in relationship to any other object that may be found in the universe, which is an intellectual leap that escapes a great many people.

3. It is certainly the case there should not be the setting of one's sights with too great a reliance in the hope that we are creatures of a rational order who have the capability of molding the emptiness of the vast universe into an element of a deep picture of our relationship to basic and fundamental existence, due to the fact that we are still in possession of many of the animal-type drives that stop us from logical thought processes as to the fact that immortality is not a spoke in the wheel of transient existence.

SUMMING UP
A Bit of Flair

A modestly elegant style includes both syntactic patterns and a choice of words that raise the passage above the ordinary. But true stylistic elegance demands a quality of thought that makes readers feel they are confronting a writer of substantial intellectual quality.

I can't tell you how to be a writer of substantial intellectual quality. Nor can I list all the words that would invest your prose with any special distinction. About the best I can do is list a few of the sentence patterns that you might experiment with when you believe your ideas merit special attention.

1. Balanced, coordinate, and parallel sentence patterns, more often after the subject than before the verb, with elements of increasing length.
2. Nominalizations toward the end of a clause, concluding with a sprinkling of prepositional phrases introduced by *of*.
3. Few, if any, sequences of N + N + N . . .
4. A few patterns of usage to signal your audience you are raising your prose to a level of formality that should command their attention. (See Lesson Ten.)

Style and Punctuation

I know there are some Persons who affect to despise it, and treat this whole Subject with the utmost Contempt, as a Trifle far below their Notice, and a Formality unworthy of their Regard: They do not hold it difficult, but despicable; and neglect it, as being above it.

Yet many learned Men have been highly sensible to its Use; and some ingenious and elegant Writers have condescended to point their Works with Care; and very eminent Scholars have not disdained to teach the Method of doing it with Propriety.

JAMES BURROW

In music, the punctuation is absolutely strict; the bars and rests are absolutely defined. But our prose cannot be quite strict, because we have to relate it to the audience. In other words we are continually changing the score.

SIR RALPH RICHARDSON

There are some punctuations that are interesting and there are some that are not.

GERTRUDE STEIN

One who uses many periods is a philosopher; many interrogations, a student; many exclamations, a fanatic.

J. L. BASFORD

F or most of us, punctuation is not an aesthetic challenge but a practical housekeeping problem: We engage it only long enough to keep things straight. And yet, deployed carefully and sensitively, commas, colons, and semicolons can make our sentences not only clear but even a bit stylish. Good punctuation won't turn a monotone into the Hallelujah Chorus, but a bit of care can produce gratifying results.

Each section of this chapter begins with the least you have to know about punctuation and then explores some of its niceties. We'll address the matter as a functional problem: How do we punctuate the beginning, the middle, and the end of a sentence? And since how we punctuate the end of a sentence most definitively comments on our basic literacy, we'll begin there.

PUNCTUATING ENDS

In Lesson Six, we distinguished two kinds of sentences: *punctuated* and *grammatical*. A *punctuated sentence* is whatever begins with a capital letter and ends with a period, question mark, or exclamation point. A *grammatical sentence* is the least we can stop with one of those marks and have nothing left over. The least a sentence can have is a finite verb, a verb that by its ending or form signals present or past. And except for imperative sentences *(Stop!)*, a grammatical sentence always provides that verb with a subject. Together, the subject and verb constitute the spine of a clause.

A clause is *independent* if it does not grammatically attach to, depend on, function as a part of any other clause. You can punctuate an independent clause as a separate sentence.

From 1925 to 1982, common stocks averaged an 8.5 percent return.

A *dependent* or *subordinate clause* usually begins with a word that signals its dependency: *because, although, if, since, when, though, after, before, as, which, who, whom, that, whether.* We usually don't punctuate a dependent clause as a separate sentence. None of these is a grammatical sentence:

Because from 1925 to 1982, common stocks averaged an 8.5 percent return.

Which from 1925 to 1982 averaged an 8.5 percent return.

> *That* from 1925 to 1982 common stocks averaged an 8.5 percent return.

When subordinate clauses such as these are punctuated as independent sentences, they are usually called "fragments." Such a clause must attach to an independent clause that precedes or follows:

> Common stocks would have been a good investment for more than the last half century, *because* from 1925 to 1982 they averaged an 8.5 percent return.

> You would have been wise to invest in common stocks, *which* from 1925 to 1982 averaged an 8.5 percent return.

> Few people are aware of this fact, *that* from 1925 to 1982 common stocks averaged an 8.5 percent return.

Another common kind of fragment begins with *-ing*.

> Stocks have been a good investment. *Averaging* an 8.5 percent return from 1925 to 1982.

The phrase beginning with *averaging* has no subject, and *averaging* is not a form of a verb that could signal past or present. It would need an *are* or *were:*

> Stocks *were* averaging an 8.5 percent return from 1925 to 1982.

If we do not provide *averaging* with a subject and a finite verb, then we have to attach it to what goes before:

> Stocks have been a good investment, *averaging* an 8.5 percent. . . .

Joining Independent Clauses

Whenever you reach the end of a grammatical sentence, including whatever dependent clauses are included in it, you can stop with a period. But you can stop less emphatically in a few other ways: First, you can use a semicolon to indicate that your first independent clause is closely linked to a second independent clause that follows the semicolon:

> In 1957 and again in 1960, Congress passed civil rights laws that remedied problems of registration and voting; *both* had significant political consequences throughout the South.

> The Beatniks were the first identifiable postwar group to reject the values of the middle-class; *subsequent* years gave us Hippies, Yippies, flower children, dropouts, communards, and Weathermen.

Second, you can end one independent clause with a comma if the next clause is also a grammatical sentence and it begins with *and, but, yet, for, so, or,* or *nor:*

> In the 1950s religion came to be viewed as a bulwark against communism, *so it* was not long after that that atheism was felt to be a threat to national security.

> American intellectuals have always followed the lead of European Marxist philosophy, *but American* academic culture has proven to be an inhospitable environment for the flourishing of communistic ideas.

It is, of course, always considered wrong to run one independent clause onto the next with no connective at all:

> The stock market is finally beginning to recover *it was* depressed for several years.

But, if clauses are relatively short, closely linked, and balanced, you can link two grammatical sentences, two independent clauses, with just a comma: Be sure that neither has any internal commas.

> Football appeals to our love for violence, *baseball* satisfies our more measured and graceful tastes.

> Women have always been underpaid, *they* are only now beginning to do something about it.

Though it is not difficult to find sentences punctuated this way in the best prose, many teachers consider this kind of punctuation incorrect, so it is wise to have a sense of your audience before you experiment.

Nor is it uncommon for writers to join two short clauses with the conjunction alone, omitting the comma:

> Oscar Wilde brazenly violated one of the fundamental laws of British society *and we* all know what happened to him.

These four ways of linking clauses—(1) semicolon, (2) comma + coordinating conjunction, (3) comma alone, and (4) conjunction alone—create an increasingly tight bond between the ideas those clauses express, so it is important that the ideas in fact be closely connected.

Special Cases: Colon and Dash

A mark of punctuation that lets you add just a slight touch of elegance is the colon: It is formal shorthand for *to illustrate, for example, for instance, that is, let me expand on what I just said, therefore, the conclusion is obvious:*

> Only one question remains to be answered: Who assumes responsibility if the project loses money?

> Dance is not one of our more widely supported art forms: Not one dance company can count on operating in the black every year, and outside of two or three major cities, we find hardly any active companies.

> Computer operators are fond of comparing their hardware to the human brain: They wax eloquent on its speed, its resourcefulness, its flexibility.

A colon also lets you balance one clause against another a bit more elegantly than with a comma or semicolon:

> Civil disobedience is the public conscience of a democracy: Mass enthusiasm is the public consensus of a tyranny.

In some contexts a dash can serve as a less formal colon—it has a kind of casual immediacy that suggests an afterthought:

> Stonehenge is one of the wonders of the ancient world—only a genius could have conceived.

(Try that with a colon—you'll sense the difference.)

You may or may not capitalize the first word in a clause following a colon: A capital letter makes what follows a bit more prominent and emphatic. Ordinarily, we don't capitalize what follows a dash.

Avoid putting a colon between a verb and a long object. Not this:

> Effective genetic counseling requires: *a thorough* knowledge of statistical genetics, an awareness of medical choices open to prospective parents, psychological competence to deal with emotional trauma.

Complete the clause before you begin a substantial list:

Effective genetic counseling requires the following preparation: *a thorough knowledge* of statistical genetics, an awareness of. . . .

PUNCTUATING BEGINNINGS

If you begin a sentence directly with a subject, you have no punctuation problems. Problems begin when you introduce a sentence with modifying words, phrases, and clauses. You can follow a few absolute rules, but more often you have to exercise good judgment.

The (almost) Absolute Rules

1. Never put a comma after an introductory subordinating conjunction such as *because, if, although, while, since, as, before, after.* Not this:

   Because, inflation is increasing faster than interest rates, people are investing their money in art objects.

2. Resist a comma after the introductory coordinating conjunctions *and, but, yet, for, so, or, nor.* Not this:

   But, we cannot know whether life on other planets realizes that we're here and simply prefers to ignore us.

   Yet, this conclusion supports that of earlier research.

Some writers who punctuate heavily will put a comma after *and, but, yet, for, so, or, nor* if an introductory word or phrase follows:

   Yet, during this period, prices continued to rise.

That is a matter of taste.

3. Generally put a comma after introductory words or phrases such as *however, nevertheless, regardless, instead, on the other hand, as a result, consequently, moreover, furthermore, that is, also, fortunately, obviously, allegedly, incidentally*—any word or phrase that comments on the whole of the following sentence:

   Furthermore, psychological studies indicate that these groups are no more neurotic or disturbed than others.

If you find yourself introducing sentence after sentence with words like these, you might consider revising a bit. A comma after just a word or two slows the pace of a sentence just when it should be gaining momentum. Too many such sentences retard the flow of the whole passage.

Four introductory words often appear without a following comma: *now, therefore, thus, hence:*

> *Now* it is clear that many constituencies will not support this position.

> *Thus* the only alternative is to choose some other action.

4. Always separate an introductory word, phrase, or clause—no matter how short—from what follows if a reader might misunderstand:

> When the lawyer concludes the opening statement from the floor may begin.

> In most cases we have treated these conditions over a period of several years.

If you open a sentence with a short introductory phrase before a short subject, you don't need a comma:

> *Once again* we find similar responses to exodermal stimuli.

> *In 1945* few returning servicemen anticipated the dramatic social changes that had transformed American society.

> *In many areas of the country* housing prices have risen twice as fast as food prices.

It's not an error to put a comma after an introductory phrase, but contemporary writers tend to use less punctuation than even those of the recent past.

Close Connections

With introductory subordinate clauses, there are some other considerations: How closely does the meaning of the introductory clause relate to the meaning of the main clause? If you open with a subordinate clause whose subject is the same as the subject of the main clause, and the meaning of one clause closely depends on the meaning of the other, you probably won't need a comma:

> When Hitler realized his Eastern front had collapsed he resolved to destroy every city through which his army would retreat.

But if the subjects of the two clauses differ and the ideas contrast, then you probably do need a comma. Compare:

> Because *we* have accepted the interpretation of the *IRS we* will drop all further appeals.

> Although *the IRS* has overruled this interpretation, *we* will continue to follow our original procedures.

Semicolons have no place between an introductory element and a subject, so you can forget about using them there. But if your subject is a long list, then try a colon or a dash followed by a summative subject. Compare:

> The President, the Vice-President, the Secretaries of the Executive Departments, the Supreme Court Justices, Senators, and members of the House of Representatives take an oath of office that pledges them to uphold the Constitution.

> The President, the Vice-President, the Secretaries of the Executive Departments, the Supreme Court Justices, Senators, and members of the House of Representatives: *all* take an oath of office that pledges them to uphold the Constitution.

> Drugs, gambling, violence, poverty, disease, despair constitute a familiar list of afflictions that destroy the fabric of a community.

> Drugs, gambling, violence, poverty, disease, despair—*they* constitute a familiar list of afflictions that destroy the fabric of a community.

Whether you choose the dash or the colon depends on how formal you want to be.

PUNCTUATING THE MIDDLE

Explaining how to punctuate inside a sentence, clause, or phrase is messy, because we have to consider nuances of grammar, meaning, and rhythm. There are, though, three principles to follow:

1. Set off with commas or dashes that which distinctly interrupts.
2. Set off with commas, dashes, or parentheses that which loosely comments on or explains essential parts of a clause or phrase.
3. Separate with commas or semicolons items in a series of three or more.

Interruptions

When you insert a phrase or clause between a subject and its verb, you usually have to set off that interruption with commas:

> Religious education, *I repeat,* is an affair of the private conscience, not of the body politic.

> The history of every animal species, *regardless of its evolutionary status,* proves that the most adaptive survive the longest.

> This one principle of TV programming, *because it simply overpowers all other considerations,* determines what each of us will watch morning, noon, and night.

(Better yet—avoid the interruptions. Move the interrupter.)

Adverbs or phrases inside a verb phrase take commas or not, depending on what your ear prefers:

> Twentieth-century poetry has *in recent years* become more comprehensible to the average reader.

> Twentieth-century poetry has, *in recent years,* become more comprehensible to the average reader.

It depends entirely on how emphatic you want to be.

If you separate a verb and its object with a phrase or word that is shorter than the object, you don't have to set it off with commas:

> In moments of great anxiety, we see *perhaps too clearly* the stuff of which our characters are made.

But if the object is considerably shorter and you want to arrange the words for the greatest impact, you might set off the interruption with a comma:

> The antagonisms between the scientific and humanistic communities have created, *in virtually every quarter of the scholarly and intellectual world,* utter distrust.

Loose Commentary

What counts as "loose commentary" depends not on grammar, but on meaning. The usual distinction is between *restrictive* and *nonrestrictive* modifiers. A nonrestrictive modifier is "loose"; it adds information to describe something that has already been identified sufficiently.
Compare these:

> It was necessary partly to reconstruct the larynx, *which had received a traumatic injury,* by means of cartilage obtained from the shoulder.

> Tax deduction dependency is awarded to *the parent with whom the child principally resides.*

Since we have only one larynx, merely naming it identifies it sufficiently. Anything more we say about it is loose, *nonrestrictive, nonspecifying* commentary, and so we set it off with commas. But since children have two parents, simply referring to one of them as *parent* doesn't identify which parent we mean. So to *parent* we add a *restrictive,* specifying modifier to identify which parent we mean. And in that case, we don't set off the modifier with commas.
Phrases and clauses that conclude a sentence should be preceded by a comma unless they are essential to the meaning of the main clause. Compare these:

> Hemingway wandered through Europe, *seeking some environment where he could write what he felt he had to.*

> Hemingway spent *most of his time seeking some environment where he could write what he felt he had to.*

> All offices will be closed from July 2 through July 6, *as announced in the daily bulletin.*

> When closing the offices, it is important *to secure all desks and safes as prescribed in Operating Manual 45-23a.*

> Those who describe what a technologically splendid future we have to look forward to usually underestimate the effect of seemingly minor social changes, *at least insofar as this country is concerned.*

> These records must *be maintained at least until the IRS has decided whether to review them.*

But, again, this is often settled by a good ear rather than a fixed rule.

In some of these cases, a dash is more casual—or striking—than a comma:

> The process was repeated a fourth time—*successfully.*

> It was necessary to fix up his voice box—*which really got hit hard*—by taking some cartilage from his shoulder.

A dash is particularly useful when the chunk of "loose commentary" has internal commas. This is just a bit confusing:

> All the nations of Central Europe, Poland, Czechoslovakia, Hungary, Roumania, Bulgaria, and Yugoslavia, have known what it is like to be in the middle of an East-West tug-of-war.

But if we set off that middle chunk with dashes, the meaning is immediately clear:

> All the nations of Central Europe—Poland, Czechoslovakia, Hungary, Roumania, Bulgaria, and Yugoslavia—have known what it is like to be in the middle of an East-West tug-of-war.

Parentheses serve much the same function as dashes, though they are usually more appropriate when you want to suggest that you are inserting a kind of *sotto voce* aside:

> The brain (if our theories are correct) is really two brains operating simultaneously.

Or explanatory information:

> Lamarck (1744–1829) was a French naturalist and pre-Darwinian evolutionist.

> The poetry of the *fin de siècle* (end of the century) period was characterized by a world-weariness and fashionable despair that was closer to intellectual vapidity than spiritual emptiness.

Series

The least complicated punctuation is that of the series. Once you decide whether or not to use a comma before the *and,* you don't have too many more decisions:

> His wit, his charm, and his appearance made him everyone's friend.

> His wit, his *charm and* his appearance made him everyone's friend.

Whichever you choose, be consistent. The advantage in always putting the comma before *and* is that your reader won't have to wonder whether the last two items are supposed to be taken as a unit or separately:

> The Treasurer will issue separate reports on the yields for Treasury notes, grain futures, common *stocks, and bonds.*

If any of the items in the series need internal commas, then use semicolons to set off the items:

> In mystery novels, the principal action ought to be economical, organic, and logical; fascinating, yet not exotic; clear, but complicated enough to hold the reader's interest—a compromise that is not always easy to strike.

How you punctuate a series of adjectives before a noun depends on whether you intend them to be rhetorically equal or increasingly specific:

> Everyone likes a big red juicy apple.

> We shall eliminate all nonfunctioning, nonrepairable, obsolete units.

Big is more general than *red, red* more general than *juicy,* so we put them in that order without commas. Compare: *a juicy red big apple.* But *nonfunctioning, nonrepairable,* and *obsolete* are equally specific, so we coordinate them with commas. Compare: *an obsolete, nonrepairable, nonfunctioning unit,* a phrase just as acceptable as the original.

Punctuating Coordinate Elements

Ordinarily, don't put a comma between just two coordinated words and phrases:

> As computers have become more sophisticated, *and more powerful,* they have taken over more *clerical, and bookkeeping* tasks.

> As computers have become more *sophisticated and more powerful,* they have taken over more *clerical and bookkeeping* tasks.

There are, however, some exceptions:

1. If you want a more intense effect, drop out the *and* and insert a comma.
   Compare:

   Abraham Lincoln never had the advantage of a formal education *and never owned* a large library.

   Abraham Lincoln never had the advantage of *a formal education, never owned* a large library.

   The great lesson of the pioneers was to stop complaining about conditions that seem difficult or even overwhelming *and to get on* with the business of shaping a life in a hostile environment.

   The great lesson of the pioneers was to stop complaining about conditions that seem difficult or even overwhelming, *to get on with* the business of shaping a life in a hostile environment.

2. A long coordinate pair occasionally needs a comma to interrupt what otherwise would be a monotonous flow:

   It is in the graveyard scene that Hamlet finally realizes that the inevitable end of all life is the grave *and that regardless* of one's station in life the end of all pretentiousness and all plotting and counterplotting must be clay.

   It is in the graveyard scene that Hamlet finally realizes that the inevitable end of all life is the grave, and that regardless of one's station in life, the end of all pretentiousness and all plotting and counterplotting must be clay.

3. Sometimes we put a comma even after a short coordinate element if we want a dramatic pause:

   These conclusions are rather thin, *and even inaccurate.*

   The ocean is one of nature's most glorious creations, *and one of its most destructive.*

   This comma is especially common before a *but:*

   Organ transplants are becoming increasingly common, *but* not less expensive.

4.   And finally, we can put a comma after a short or long coordinate element if its absence might mislead our reader about the grammar of a sentence:

> Conrad's *Heart of Darkness* inquires into those primitive impulses that lie deep in each of us and stir only in our darkest dreams and asserts the unassailable need for the civilized values and institutions that control those impulses.

A comma after *dreams* would clearly mark the end of one coordinate member and the beginning of the next:

> Conrad's *Heart of Darkness* inquires into those primitive impulses that lie deep in each of us and stir only in our darkest dreams, *and asserts* the unassailable need for the civilized values and institutions that control those impulses.

Exercise 9-1

Here are two passages minus all their original punctuation. Extra spacings indicate boundaries of grammatical sentences. Punctuate these passages twice, once using the least punctuation possible, then a second time using as much varied punctuation as you can. Then do it a third time in the way that you think most effective.

1.   From all available evidence no black man had ever set foot in this tiny Swiss village before I came   I was told before arriving that I would probably be a "sight" for the village   I took this to mean that people of my complexion were rarely seen in Switzerland and also that people are always something of a "sight" outside the city   it did not occur to me possibly because I am an American that there could be people anywhere who had never seen a Negro   it is a fact that cannot be explained on the basis of the   inaccessibility of the village   the village is very high   but it is only four hours from Milan and three hours from Lausanne   it is true that it is virtually unknown   few people making plans for a holiday would elect to come here   on the other hand the villagers are able presumably to come and go as they please which they do to another town at the foot of the mountain with a population of approximately five thousand the nearest place to see a movie or go to the bank   in the village there is no movie house no bank no library no theater very few radios one jeep one station wagon and at the moment one typewriter mine

an invention which the woman next door to me here had never seen
    there are about six hundred people living here all Catholic   I
conclude this from the fact that the Catholic church is open all year
round whereas the Protestant chapel set off on a hill a little removed
from the village is open only in the summertime when the tourists
arrive   there are four or five hotels all closed now and four or five
bistros of which however only two do any business during the winter
    these two do not do a great deal   for life in the village seems to
end around nine or ten o'clock   there are a few stores butcher baker
épicerie, a hardware store and a moneychanger who cannot change
travelers' checks but must send them down to the bank an operation
which takes two or three days   there is something called the Ballet
Hall closed in the winter and used for God knows what certainly not
ballet in the summer   there seems to be only one schoolhouse in
the village and this for the quite young children
        —James Baldwin, "Stranger in the Village," from *Notes of a Native Son*

2. In fact of course the notion of universal knowledge has always been
    an illusion   but it is an illusion fostered by the monistic view of the
    world in which a few great central truths determine in all its wonder-
    ful and amazing proliferation everything else that is true   we are
    not today tempted to search for these keys that unlock the whole of
    human knowledge and of man's experience   we know that we are
    ignorant   we are well taught it   and the more surely and deeply
    we know our own job the better able we are to appreciate the full
    measure of our pervasive ignorance   we know that these are
    inherent limits compounded no doubt and exaggerated by that sloth
    and that complacency without which we would not be men at all
    but knowledge rests on knowledge   what is new is meaningful
    because it departs slightly from what was known before   this is a
    world of frontiers where even the liveliest of actors or observers will
    be absent most of the time from most of them   perhaps this sense
    was not so sharp in the village that village which we have learned a
    little about but probably do not understand too well the village of
    slow change and isolation and fixed culture which evokes our nostal-
    gia even if not our full comprehension   perhaps in the villages men
    were not so lonely   perhaps they found in each other a fixed
    community a fixed and only slowly growing store of knowledge of a
    single world   even that we may doubt   for there seem to be
    always in the culture of such times and places vast domains of
    mystery if not unknowable then imperfectly known endless and open
        —J. Robert Oppenheimer, "The Sciences and Man's Community," from *Science
                                            and The Common Understanding*

SUMMING UP
Reasonable Punctuation

1. At the end of a grammatical sentence, use one of the following.
   a. A period, question mark, or exclamation point, even if the next sentence begins with *and, but, yet, for, so, or, nor:*

   At first, the group was strangely unresponsive. *But* as the meeting progressed, they became more animated.

   b. A semicolon, if the next grammatical sentence does not begin with *and, but, yet, for, so, or, nor:*

   Imagination is not a literary gift; *it* is part of being a human being.

   c. A comma, if the next grammatical sentence begins with *and, but, yet, for, so, or, nor:*

   It is true, as Marshall McLuhan says, that the medium is the message, *but* it is also true that the message is considerably more than just the medium.

But if the first grammatical sentence has a good deal of internal punctuation, use a semicolon before the conjunction:

   In the sciences, new facts, new theories, are not merely added to the sum of knowledge, regardless of how long and how established that sum of knowledge might be; *nor* do those new facts and new theories merely replace the old, as a new brick completely fills the space of one that has been removed and discarded.

   d. A colon if what follows the colon is a list, or a restatement, consequence, conclusion, or illustration of the first sentence:

   Harry Truman entered office as one of the least promising of our presidents: He had been a minor senator from Missouri, an obedient political partyman, and someone who Roosevelt believed would best serve his country by presiding over the Senate, quietly.

   e. Just a comma if the grammatical sentences are short, do not contain internal punctuation, and are closely related and rhetorically balanced:

I came, I saw, I went away impressed.

f. Just an *and, but, yet, so, for, or, nor* if the grammatical sentences are short and balanced:

American fishermen argued for a 200-mile limit *and* the American public supported them.

More tried to turn Einstein into a political pundit *but* he would have none of it.

Compare:

Texas and Louisiana have requested that Mexico pay for the recent oil spill that polluted their coasts and damaged their fishing and tourist industry, *but* Mexico has flatly refused.

No public official has the right to set him- or herself above the law, *and* it's clear that the American public is not about to change that principle.

g. A dash, if the following grammatical sentence is short and dramatic:

We are all a product of our environment—so why do we abuse it?

2.   At the beginning of a grammatical sentence, punctuate as follows:
a. If the sentence begins with a subordinate clause, put no punctuation after the subordinating conjunction:

Although academic freedom prevents the state from using the educational system for its own ends, it cannot be invoked to allow teachers to preach religion or politics in the classroom.

b. Nothing after *and, but, yet, for, so, nor, or*. Not:

Both Kennedy and Nixon were qualified to be President in 1960. *But,* Kennedy knew how to manipulate the media more effectively.

c. A comma after a word or phrase that relates to the whole of the following sentence:

Therefore, to appreciate ballet is to appreciate both animal grace and the grace of intellect.

d. A comma if your reader can mistake the grammar of a sentence. Not:

If you want to improve your mind and your soul must be disciplined.

e. A comma after a long (more than six or so words) introductory element:

Regardless of any appearance of random or even accidental form, a work of modern art always implies a deliberate intention.

f. A dash or a colon between a subject consisting of a list and a word that summarizes the list:

Copernicus, Galileo, Newton, Darwin, Freud, Einstein—they did not give us new and unfamiliar things to look at so much as new ways to look at familiar things.

The freedom to travel, to worship, to read what we will, to gather and discuss the conduct of our lives: Such privileges are unknown in most of the world.

3. Inside a sentence, punctuate as follows:
   a. Set off obvious interruptions with commas or dashes:

The women's movement—*I use the term loosely and inclusively*—has brought together many women who otherwise never would have met.

A nation, *they say,* gets the government it deserves.

b. Set off parenthetical, nonrestrictive, loosely added material with commas, with parentheses (infrequently), or with dashes (even less frequently):

Toscanini, *who assuredly will be remembered as the premier maestro of the twentieth century,* never exaggerated his own abilities.

During this period (*from roughly the middle of June to the end of summer*), Allied forces advanced very slowly.

Every ruler—*king, president, prime minister, or tyrant*—surrounds himself with advisers who will assure him he is always right.

c. Separate items in a list with commas, or if those items are themselves punctuated with commas, with semicolons:

This will require money, effort, and time.

I shall first discuss Hamlet, a tragedy of the intellect; then Lear, a tragedy of the heart; and finally Macbeth, a tragedy of the soul.

4. Separate two coordinated items with a comma under the following conditions.
   a. When the beginning of the second element can be mistaken for a continuation of the first:

We must continue to believe that we can shape our future and achieve our goal, and resolutely dedicate ourselves to that effort.

   b. When the first item is so long that its rhythm becomes monotonous:

Myths constitute the record of those prehistorical events that have given shape to a preliterate culture, and give dramatic power to the cultural values that hold that shape.

   c. When you want to dramatize the second element:

We must never underestimate the power of an aroused citizenry, or over-estimate it.

Style and Usage

It is not the business of grammar, as some critics seem preposterously to imagine, to give law to the fashions which regulate our speech. On the contrary, from its conformity to these, and from that alone, it derives all its authority and value.

GEORGE CAMPBELL

No grammatical rules have sufficient authority to control the firm and established usage of language. Established custom, in speaking and writing, is the standard to which we must at last resort for determining every controverted point in language and style.

HUGH BLAIR

English usage is sometimes more than mere taste, judgment, and education—sometimes it's sheer luck, like getting across the street.

E. B. WHITE

God does not much mind bad grammar, but He does not take any particular pleasure in it.

ERASMUS

So far, we've discussed matters of choice: From among sentences that might all express the same idea, how do we pick the best one? We might reject

There was an insufficiency of comptroller research support.

for

The comptroller did not support our research sufficiently.

But we wouldn't say that the first was grammatically wrong, only less forceful and direct than it could be.

At first glance, we might think that, "good" grammar, and proper usage are an altogether different matter. When we read in the *American Heritage Dictionary* that *irregardless* is "nonstandard... never acceptable" (except when we're trying to be funny), the possibility of choosing between *irregardless* and *regardless* may seem at best academic. *Regardless* versus *irregardless* isn't a matter of better and worse but of right and utterly, irredeemably wrong.

That seems to simplify matters: To choose correctly, we don't need good taste or sound judgment, only a reliable memory. If we remember that *irregardless* is always and everywhere wrong, then *irregardless* does not even rise to the level of conscious decision. We have only to memorize the same kind of prescriptions for a host of other items:

— Don't begin a sentence with *and* or *but.*
— Don't end a sentence with a preposition.
— Don't split infinitives.
— Don't use double negatives.

Unfortunately, questions of usage are not quite that simple: A good many of the grammatical rules we find in some dictionaries and in some handbooks of usage have little or no basis in linguistic fact. Other social rules of usage are imperatives that we violate at the risk of seeming at least badly educated. And then there are rules that we can observe or not, depending on the effect we want.

It's important to keep in mind that we're discussing here not spoken, but written English. The English-speaking world has a variety of spoken dialects, each different from the others in pronunciation, vocabulary, and grammar. Despite what some may think about a "pure Boston English" as opposed to "illiterate Ozark," no local spoken dialect is inherently better—

or worse—than the standard dialect spoken in any other part of our country. Every region has a prestige dialect that careful speakers use on those occasions when careful speech is important. And each dialect has its own distinctive features of pronunciation, word choice, and grammar.

But written English is different. For better or worse, all parts of the English-speaking world have tacitly agreed on most of the conventions that define careful standard written English. Different parts of the native English-speaking world may spell a few words in different ways: *theatre* versus *theater, gaol* versus *jail, colour* versus *color,* and so on. We may differ on a very few small points of grammar: I *have no money* versus *I don't have any money.* And in different parts of the world, we may have different words for roughly the same things: *dust bin* versus *garbage can, attorney* and *barrister* versus *lawyer,* and so on. But for the most part, native speakers of English observe a written standard that is far more uniform than the standard among local spoken dialects. This development of a written standard occurs in every literate society.

rules and RULES

To the end of creating this standard written English, grammarians and teachers of English have, over the last few hundred years, assembled a variety of prescriptions and proscriptions whose observance, they believe, distinguishes writers who are careful and responsible from those who are not. The rules range from where to put a comma, to how to use *disinterested* and *uninterested,* to the proper case of a pronoun after *is.* But these rules have been hoarded up less on the basis of their intrinsic logical force or on principles of inherent clarity and precision, than on grounds that have been largely idiosyncratic, historically accidental. No universal principle of logic or experience demands that the past tense of *know* be *knew* rather than *knowed,* or that *like* be now and forevermore a preposition, never a conjunction.

As one consequence of this largely random accumulation, not all rules of usage have equal standing with all writers of English, even all careful writers of English. A very few especially fastidious writers and editors have accepted and try to observe every rule. Most careful writers observe fewer, because they have never had all the rules imposed on them by all their editors or teachers, no matter how critical and careful those writers might be in other matters. There are also writers who know the rules, but who also know that not all of them are worth observing and that other rules should be observed only on certain occasions.

Whether we choose to be absolutely safe or rhetorically selective depends on both our competence and our confidence. We could adopt the worst case approach: We learn and observe all the rules all the time because somewhere, sometime, someone might condemn us for beginning a sentence with *and* or ending it with *up,* and so we keep a stack of grammar books and usage manuals close by to consult as we edit—painfully—every line we write, until we have memorized the rules so thoroughly that we obey them without thought. But once we do that, we may have deprived ourselves of a valuable stylistic flexibility. And sooner or later, we will impose those rules—valid or not—on others. After all, what good is learning a rule if all we can do is obey it?

But careful selectivity has its problems too, because that requires us to learn which rules to ignore and which to observe—and when. It also demands the confidence to face up to those who consider a deliberately split infinitive or a singular *data* as a sign of careless writing—or deliberate scorn of careful writing.

An attitude short of blind obedience to every rule in every grammar book need not indicate a bad education or a contemptuous mind: We may reject some rules once we recognize how the best writers write—not how they *say* they write, but how they *do* write. If otherwise careful, educated, and intelligent writers of first-rate prose do not avoid ending a sentence with a preposition, then regardless of what some grammarians or editors would say, a preposition at the end of a sentence is *not* an error of usage.

The standard adopted here is not that of Transcendental Correctness. It derives from the observable habits of those we could never accuse of having sloppy minds or of deliberately writing careless prose. On the basis of that principle, we can recognize four kinds of "rules." The kinds are simple enough: What's less clear is which rules go in which category.

Real Rules

The first—the most important—category of rules includes those whose violation would unequivocally brand you as a writer of nonstandard English. Here are a few:

1. Double negatives: The engine had *hardly no* systematic care.
2. Nonstandard verb forms: They *knowed* that nothing would happen.
3. Double comparatives: This procedure is *more better.*
4. Some adjectives for adverbs: They did the work *real good.*
5. Redundant subjects: *These ideas, they* need explanation.

6. Certain incorrect pronoun forms: *Him* and *me* will study the problem.
7. Some subject-verb disagreements: *They was* ready to begin.

There are others. But they are so egregious that most of you already know that they are never violated by educated writers. And because these rules are observed in even casual writing, their observance passes unremarked: They is rules whose violation we instantly notes, but whose observance we entirely ignore.

Nonrules

A second group of rules includes those whose observance we do not remark, and whose violation we do not remark either. In fact, these are not rules at all, but a species of folklore, widely enforced by many editors and schoolteachers, but largely ignored by most educated and careful writers. What follows is based on a good deal of time spent reading prose that is carefully written and intended to be carefully read. I can assert only that the "rules" listed below are violated so consistently that, unless we indict for bad grammar just about every serious writer of modern English, we have to reject as misinformed anyone who would try to enforce them.[1]

1. "Never begin a sentence with a coordinating conjunction such as *and* or *but.*" Allegedly, not this:

   > *But,* it will be asked, is tact not an individual gift, therefore highly variable in its choices? *And* if that is so, what guidance can a manual offer, other than that of its author's prejudices—mere impressionism?
   >
   > —Wilson Follett, *Modern American Usage: A Guide,* edited and completed by Jacques Barzun et al.

2. "Never begin a sentence with *because.*" Allegedly, not this:

   > *Because* we have access to so much historical fact, today we know a good deal about changes within the humanities which were not apparent to those in any age much before our own and which the individual scholar must constantly reflect on.
   >
   > —Walter Ong, S. J., "The Expanding Humanities and the Individual Scholar," *PMLA*

---

[1]Each citation offered as an example of a "rule" violated is in its original form, except for the italics, which I have added.

but presumably this:

Since we have access to so much historical fact, today we. . . .

or

We have access to much historical fact. *Consequently* today we. . . .

Although this proscription appears in no handbook of usage I know of, it seems to have popular currency. It must stem from advice intended to avoid sentence fragments like this one:

The application was rejected. *Because the deadline had passed.*

When the *because*-clause that opens a sentence is followed by a main clause, and punctuated so that the two constitute a single punctuated sentence, then it is entirely correct:

Because the deadline had passed, the application was rejected.

3.   "When referring to an inanimate referent, use the relative pronoun *that*—not *which*—for restrictive clauses; use *which* for nonrestrictive clauses." Allegedly not this:

Next is a typical situation *which* a practiced writer corrects "for style" virtually by reflex action.

Jacques Barzun, Simple and Direct

But presumably this:

Next is a typical situation *that* a practiced writer corrects "for style" virtually by reflex action.

Both are entirely correct.

4.   "Use *each other* to refer to two, *one another* to refer to three or more." Allegedly, not this:

Now "society" is ever in search of novelty—and it is a limited body of well-to-do women and men of leisure. From the almost exclusive association of these persons with *each other,* there arises a kind of special vocabulary, which is constantly changing. . . .

—James B. Greenough and George L. Kittredge, Words and Their Ways
in English Speech

But presumably this:

> From the almost exclusive association of these persons with *one another,* there arises a kind of special vocabulary. . . .

One another for more than two may be just a shade more formal than *each other,* but neither phrase is, in good usage, limited in the way the rule states.

5. "Use *between* with two, *among* with three or more." Allegedly, not this:

> . . . government remained in the hands of fools and adventurers, foreigners and fanatics, who *between* them went near to wrecking the work of the Tudor monarchy. . . .
> —Geo. Macaulay Trevelyan, *A Shortened History of England*

But presumably this:

> . . . government remained in the hands of fools and adventurers, foreigners and fanatics, who *among* them went near to wrecking the work of the Tudor monarchy. . . .

Among goes with three or more, of course, but *between* also occurs in that context.

6. "Don't use *which* or *this* to refer to a whole clause." Allegedly, not this:

> Although the publishers have not yet destroyed the plates of the second edition of Merriam-Webster's unabridged dictionary, they do not plan to keep it in print, *which* is a pity.
> —Dwight MacDonald, "The String Untuned," *The New Yorker*

But presumably this:

> Although the publishers have not yet destroyed the plates . . . they do not plan to keep it in print, *a decision which* is a pity.

Occasionally, this kind of construction can be ambiguous. In the next example, is it the letter that makes her happy, or the fact that it was given to her?

We gave her the letter, which made her happy.

Here, a summative modifier makes the meaning unambiguous:

We gave her the letter, *a thoughtful act* that made her happy.

When it is clear what the *which* refers to, this kind of broad reference is entirely acceptable.

7. "Use *fewer* with nouns you can count, *less* with quantities you cannot." Allegedly, not this:

> I can remember no *less than five occasions* when the correspondence columns of *The Times* rocked with volleys of letters from the academic profession protesting that academic freedom is in danger and the future of scholarship threatened.
> —Noel Gilroy Annan, Lord Annan, "The Life of the Mind in British Universities Today," *ACLS Newsletter*

But presumably this:

> I can remember no *fewer than five* occasions when. . . .

It is true that *fewer* is restricted to countable nouns. But *less* now frequently occurs with countable nouns in the prose of many who certainly qualify as careful writers.

8. "Use *due to,* meaning 'because of,' only in a phrase that modifies a noun, never in a phrase that modifies a verb." Allegedly, not this:

> . . . cooperation between the Department of Economics and the Business School and between the Business School and the Law School will be much greater ten years from now than at present, *due to* the personal relations of the younger men on the three faculties.
> —James Bryant Conant, The *President's Report:* 1951–1952, Harvard University Press

But presumably this:

> . . . cooperation will be much greater ten years from now than at present, *because of* the personal relations of the younger men on the three faculties.

There are also a few individual words whose usage is proscribed by extremely conservative teachers and editors. But the actual use of these words by careful writers is, as a rule, unremarked by equally careful readers.

Most careful writers use *since* with the meaning of "because"; *alternative* to refer to one of three or more choices; *anticipate* to mean "expect"; *continuous* for *continual* and vice versa; *contact* as a general verb meaning "communicate with." Though *data* and *media* as singulars are *bêtes noires* for some observers, they are used as singular nouns by large numbers of careful writers, in the same way they use *agenda* and *insignia.* (*Strata, errata,* and *criteria* still seem to be plurals for most careful writers.) *Infer* for *imply* and *disinterested* for *uninterested* are countenanced by some standard dictionaries whose editors base their decisions on the usage of careful writers. Many teachers and editors disagree.

In the most formal of circumstances, circumstances in which you would want to avoid the slightest hint of violating even the most trivial point of usage, you might decide to observe all these rules (excepting 1 and 2). In most ordinary circumstances, though, they are ignored by most careful writers. If you decide to adopt the worst-case approach and observe them all, all the time—well, to each his own. Private virtues are their own reward.

Optional Rules

These next rules complement the first group: For the most part, few readers will notice if you violate them. But when you observe them, you will signal a level of formality that few careful readers will miss.

1.   "Never split an infinitive." Some purists would condemn Dwight MacDonald, a linguistic archconservative, for writing this:

> . . . one wonders why Dr. Gove and his editors did not think of labelling *knowed* as substandard right where it occurs, and one suspects that they wanted *to slightly conceal* the fact or at any rate to put off its exposure as long as decently possible.
>
> —"The String Untuned," *The New Yorker*

They would require this:

> . . . one wonders why Dr. Gove and his editors did not think of labelling *knowed* as substandard right where is occurs, and one suspects that they wanted *to conceal the fact slightly* or at any rate to put off its exposure as long as decently possible.

But the split infinitive is now so common among the very best writers that when we make an effort to avoid splitting it, we invite notice, whether we intend to or not.

2.   "Use *shall* as the first person simple future, *will* for second and third person simple future; use *will* to mean strong intention in the first person, *shall* for second and third person." Some purists would condemn F. L. Lucas for writing this:

I *will* end with two remarks by two wise old women of the civilized eighteenth century.
—"What Is Style?" *Holiday*

They would demand:

I *shall* end with two remarks by two wise old women of the civilized eighteenth century.

They would be mistaken to do so.

3.   "Always use *whom* as the object of a verb or preposition." Purists would condemn William Zinsser for writing this:

Soon after you confront this matter of preserving your identity, another question will occur to you: "*Who* am I writing for?"
—*On Writing Well*

They would insist on:

Soon after you confront this matter of preserving your identity, another question will occur to you: "For *whom* am I writing?"

Whom is a small but distinct flag of conscious correctness, especially when the *whom* is in fact wrong:

We found a candidate *whom* we thought was most qualified.

The rule: The form of the pronoun depends on whether it is a subject or an object of its own clause. Since *who* is the subject of *was* in

We found a candidate ⌐ we thought *who* was most qualified.

who is the correct form, not *whom*. In this next example, *whom* is the object of *overlooked:*

We found a candidate ⌐ we thought we had overlooked.   *whom*

If you are in doubt about the matter, try dropping the *who/whom* altogether:

We found a candidate we thought we had overlooked.

4. "Never end a sentence with a preposition." Purists, presumably, would condemn Sir Ernest Gowers for this:

> The peculiarities of legal English are often used as a stick to beat the official *with*.
>
> — *The Complete Plain Words*

And insist on this:

> The peculiarities of legal English are often used as a stick *with which* to beat the official.

The second is more formal than the first, but the first is still correct. In fact, whenever we move a preposition before its object, we make the sentence a bit more formal. And any obligatory *whom* after the preposition only compounds the formality.

Compare:

> The man *with whom* I spoke was not the man *to whom* I had been referred.

> The man I spoke *with* was not the man I had been referred *to*.

5. "Do not use *whose* as the possessive pronoun for an inanimate referent." Purists would correct I. A. Richards for this:

> And, on other occasions, the meaning comes from other partly parallel uses, *whose* relevance we can feel, without necessarily being able to state it explicitly.
>
> — *The Philosophy of Rhetoric*

They would change it to this:

> And, on other occasions, the meaning comes from other partly parallel uses, the relevance *of which* we can feel, without necessarily being able to state it explicitly.

6. "Use *one* as a generalized pronoun instead of *you*." Purists would revise Monroe Beardsley's:

When explicit meanings are wrongly combined, *you* get a logical fault (this is oversimplifying somewhat, but take it as a first approximation).

—"Style and Good Style," *Reflections on High School English: NDEA Institute Lectures,* ed. Gary Tate

into the more stilted:

When explicit meanings are wrongly combined, *one* gets a logical fault (this is oversimplifying somewhat, but *one* may take it as a first approximation).

7.   "Do not refer to *one* with *he* or *his;* repeat *one.*" Purists would deplore Theodore Bernstein's usage:

Thus, unless one belongs to that tiny minority who can speak directly and beautifully, *one* should not write as *he* talks.

—*The Careful Writer*

They would prefer the more formal:

Thus, unless *one* belongs to that tiny minority who can speak directly and beautifully, *one* should not write as *one* talks.

8.   "When expressing a contrary-to-fact statement, use the subjunctive form of the verb." Purists would deny H. W. Fowler this:

Another suffix that is not a living one, but is sometimes treated as if it *was,* is *-al; &.* . . .

—*A Dictionary of Modern English Usage*

They would insist upon:

Another suffix that is not a living one, but is sometimes treated as if it *were,* is *-al; &.* . . .

As the English subjunctive quietly fades into linguistic history, it leaves a residue of forms infrequent enough to impart to a sentence a slightly archaic—and therefore formal—tone. We regularly use the simple past tense to express most subjunctives:

If we *knew* what to do, we *would* do it.

Be is the problem: Strictly construed, the subjunctive demands *were,* but *was* is gradually replacing it:

If this *were* 1941, a loaf of bread would cost twenty cents.

If this *was* 1941, a loaf of bread would cost twenty cents.

Certainly, when the occasion calls for sonorous formal English, the wise writer chooses the formal usage. But in all these cases, the writer **chooses.**

Special Formality

The list of items that create a special sense of formality might include a few that don't involve disputed points of usage, but do let you elevate your style a bit above the ordinary.

1.   Negative inversion. Probably the most famous negative inversion is President John F. Kennedy's

> *Ask not* what your country can do for you, ask what you can do for your country.

> Compare:

> Do not ask what your country can do for you, . . .

Negatives such as *rarely, never, not, only,* and so on, typically let you put an auxilliary verb before its subject:

> *Never have* so many owed so much to so few.

> *Rarely do* we confront a situation such as this.

> *Only once has* this corporation failed to pay a dividend.

2.   Conditional inversion. Instead of beginning a conditional clause with *if,* begin it with *should, were,* or *had.*
       Compare:

> *If* anyone should question the grounds on which this decision was made, we can point to centuries of tradition.

> *Should* anyone question the grounds on which this decision was made, we can point to centuries of tradition.

> *If* there had been any objections, they would have been met.

> *Had* there been any objections, they would have been met.

If I were prepared to answer you now, I should do so happily.

Were I prepared to answer you now, I should do so happily.

3.   Instead of *do not have to,* use *need not:*

You *don't have to* answer now.

You *need not* answer now.

4.   Instead of *does not have* any, use *have no:*

The court *does not have* any precedent to follow.

The court *has no* precedent to follow.

Bêtes Noires

For some, one group of rules has become the object of special reverence. Why such feeling should be invested in these particular items is difficult to explain: They have probably become the symbolic flags around which those most intensely concerned with linguistic purity (whatever that may be) have tacitly agreed to rally. None of the items interferes with clarity and concision; indeed, some of them let us save a word here and there. But for one reason or another, they arouse such intense ire in so many editors, teachers, and ordinary citizens that you should be aware of their special status.

1.   Never use *like* for *as* or *as if.* Not this:

These operations failed *like* the earlier ones did.

It looks *like* we require further data on this matter.

But this:

These operations failed *as* the earlier ones did.

It looks *as if* we require further data on this matter.

2.   After *different,* use *from,* never *to* or *than.* Not this:

These numbers are *different than* the others.

I must solve this problem *differently than* I did last year.

But this:

These numbers are *different from* the others.

I must solve this problem *differently from the way* I did last year.

3. Use *hopefully* only when the subject of the sentence is in fact hopeful. Not this:

Hopefully, the matter will be resolved soon.

But this:

I hopefully say that the matter will be resolved soon.

4. Never qualify *unique* or *perfect* with a *very, rather, quite, somewhat,* etc. Not this:

A *very unique* product was developed by his company.

(One wonders what the Founding Fathers would have said to someone who criticized "We the People of the United States, in order to form a more perfect union, . . .")

5. Never use *finalize* to mean *finish, complete, end.*
6. Never use *irregardless* to mean *regardless.*

A Special Problem: Pronouns and Sexism

We expect verbs to agree with their subjects. Not this:

There *is* several *reasons* for this.

But this:

There *are* several *reasons* for this.

So do we ordinarily expect pronouns to agree in number with what they refer to. Not this:

The early *efforts* to oppose the building of a hydrogen bomb failed because *it* was not coordinated with the scientific and political communities. *No one* was willing to step forth and expose *themselves* to the anti-Communist hysteria unless *they* had the backing of others.

But this:

> The early *efforts* to oppose the building of a hydrogen bomb failed
> because *they* were not coordinated with the scientific and political com-
> munities. *No one* was willing to step forth and expose *himself* to the
> anti-Communist hysteria unless *he* had the backing of others.

There are two problems here. The first is whether to use a singular or
plural noun when you refer to a singular noun that is plural in meaning:
group, committee, staff, administration, and so on. Some writers use a
singular pronoun when the group acts as a single entity:

> The *committee* has met but has not yet made *its* decision.

But when the members of the group act individually, we always use a plural
pronoun:

> The *committee* received the memo, but not all of *them* have read it.

These days we find the plural used in both senses.

The second problem is whether to use a masculine or a feminine
pronoun to refer to indefinite pronouns like *someone, everyone, no one*
and to nouns that do not indicate gender: *a teacher, a person, a student.*

> *Everyone* who spends four years in college realizes what a soft life *they*
> had only when *they* get a nine-to-five job, with no summer and Christmas
> vacations.

> When *a person* gets involved with drugs, no one can help *them* unless
> *they* want to help *themselves.*

In both cases, more formal usage requires the singular pronoun:

> *Everyone* who spends four years in college realizes what a soft life *he* had
> only when *he* gets a nine-to-five job, with no summer and Christmas
> vacations.

> When *a person* gets involved with drugs, no one can help *him* unless *he*
> wants to help *himself.*

But when we observe the formal rule, we raise another, thornier
problem—the matter of sexist language.

Obviously, what we perceive to be our social responsibilities and the sensitivities of our audience must always come first: Many believe that we lose little, and gain much, by substituting *humankind* for *mankind, police officer* for *policeman, synthetic* for *man-made,* etc. (Those who ask whether we should also substitute *personhole cover* for *manhole cover,* or *person-in-the-moon* for *man-in-the-moon,* either miss the point, or are making a tendentious one.) And if we are writing for an audience that might judge our language sexist, then sheer common sense demands that we find ways to express our ideas in nonsexist ways, even at the cost of a little wordiness. We do little harm when we substitute for *The Dawn of Man* something like *The Dawn of Human Society.*

But a generic *he* is different: If we reject *he* as a generic pronoun because it is sexist, and *they* to refer to indefinite singulars because it is diffuse or potentially ambiguous (its formal "grammaticality" aside), we are left with either a clumsily intrusive *he or she* or an imperative to rewrite sentence after sentence in arbitrary and sometimes awkward ways.

Now, no one with even the dullest ear for style can choose the first alternative without flinching:

> When a writer does not consider the ethnicity of his or her readers, they may respond in ways he or she would not have anticipated to certain words that for him or her are entirely innocent of ethnic bias.

So we have to rewrite. We can begin by substituting something for the singular *his,* perhaps plurals:

> When a *writer* does not consider the ethnicity of *his* readers . . .

> When *writers* do not consider the ethnicity of *their* readers . . .

We can also try passives, nominalizations, and other phrases that let us drop pronouns altogether:

> *Failure to consider* a reader's ethnic background may result in an *unexpected response* to certain words that the writer considers entirely innocent of ethnic bias.

When it's appropriate, we can always try switching the pronoun from a third person *he* to a second person *you* or a first person *we:*

> If *we* do not consider the ethnic background of *our* readers, *they* may

respond in ways *we* would not expect to certain words that to *us* are entirely innocent of ethnic bias.

Finally, we can use *she* where we might otherwise use a *he,* as I have done in this book.

Finally, each of us has to decide whether the social consequences of a sexist *he* justify the effort required to avoid it and the occasionally graceless or even diffuse style that such an effort can produce. No one committed to writing the clearest, most fluent and precise prose can fail to recognize the value of a generic *he:* It lets us begin a sentence briskly and smoothly; it lets us assign to a verb specific agency; it lets us avoid ambiguity, diffuseness, and abstraction.

But for the kind of writing that most of us do, nuances of phrasing and cadence so fine may well be less important than the social value of unqualified nonsexist language. Its cost is a few moments' thought and an occasionally self-conscious sentence; that cost is slight.

precision and PRECISION

You may assign some of the items taken up in this Lesson to categories different from those I have suggested. Some readers would add many other points of usage. And some would insist that every one of those items, and many more besides, belong in that first category, those constructions that invariably distinguish civilized speakers and writers of standard English from those who are not. If we don't respect all of these rules, they argue, we begin the slide down the slippery slope into national inarticulateness.

The impulse to regulate—and by regulating, fix—language has a long tradition, not only in the English-speaking world, but in literate cultures everywhere. We invest a great deal of ourselves in learning our forms of speech, and then in mastering the fine points that, we are told, distinguish careful, responsible English from the language of those who are crude, careless, and unreliable. We believe that both our language and our values are threatened when we hear others use forms different from those we use, especially when those others may seem also to have values that threaten ours.

We usually express our linguistic values as a passionate concern for "precision," for maintaining "standards." Unless we maintain those standards, some argue, our language will degenerate into a barbarousness unequal to the needs of cultured discourse. But since no language has ever been known to "degenerate" into a form that defeats effective communication, it is unlikely ours ever will.

We can put this matter of precision more usefully like this: If we ignore imprecise and clumsy writing, people will go on writing clumsily and imprecisely—in all the ways we've been discussing. And if they go on writing clumsily and imprecisely, then eventually clumsiness and imprecision will become the accepted standard of written discourse. And when that happens, clumsy and imprecise thinking cannot be far behind. *That* is a matter worth some passion.

The trouble begins when we try to define the object of our passion, for, of course, we need examples of imprecise and clumsy writing that we can hold up for public abuse. But not many of us are going to memorize for this purpose good examples of bad writing. (And even if we did, they would have no general use: Who writes the same sentence twice?) We find it easier to assemble a list of stock items that we can cite as reliable examples of careless writing. When the same items have been steadily abused for two and a half centuries, they become not just random items of disputed usage but symbols of the careful writer's dedication to the quality of her product. That's why, on TV talk shows and in newspapers and magazines, critics who deplore the declining state of the language always rehearse the same stock errors: *like* for *as, different than* for *different from, disinterested* for *uninterested, finalize, hopefully,* etc. These items have become the instantly recognized symbols of what we say we are fighting against in our determination to defend precise language. In fact, if tomorrow every writer of English began to observe every rule of usage, no matter how trivial, we should have to invent new ones, for their universal observance would substantially improve the language not at all, and it would deprive of their stock examples those for whom the purity of English is a special passion.

Most of us who are committed to excellence in prose share a common end: a style that communicates effectively, even elegantly when elegance is appropriate. And that style, by and large, is a style that is clear, precise, and forceful. Some believe that we shall achieve that end only if we include in our definition of precision a precise adherence to all the rules of usage. Others do not. Wherever you decide to take your stand, keep this in mind: A writer who faithfully observes every one of these rules can still write wretched prose. And some of the most lucid, precise, and educated prose is written by those for whom *some* of these rules have no force whatsoever.

SUMMING UP
The Uses of Idiosyncrasy

Because usage is largely a matter of personal taste—idiosyncratic, individual, unpredictable—I can offer no broad generalizations, no global principle by which to decide any given item. Indeed, if usage did submit to logical analysis and generalization—to systematic analogy, usage would be no issue, for most "errors" of usage result when a speaker or writer extends a regularity too far: When a speaker applies the past tense rule once too often, he produces the entirely logical *knowed*. The same impulse leads to other "errors": *hisself* and *theirselves, ain't* as a perfectly logical and historically correct contraction of *am not, data* is a singular, since it lacks a plural number -*s*. Indeed, the social utility of idiosyncratic rules is precisely in their idiosyncrasy. It guarantees that only those with the leisure and inclination to learn them will do so.

Finally, I think, we choose among these items less on the basis of their real or supposed correctness than according to a sense of our own personal style. Some of us are straightforward and plainspeaking; others take pleasure in a bit of elegance, of fastidiously self-conscious "class." The *shalls* and the *wills,* the *whos* and the *whoms,* the self-consciously unsplit infinitives—they are the small choices that let those of us who wish to do so express that sense of linguistic conservatism that many believe testifies to their linguistic precision.

Some Terms Defined

Grammar is the ground of all.
WILLIAM LANGLAND

There is a satisfactory boniness about grammar which the flesh of sheer vocabulary requires before it can become vertebrate and walk the earth. But to study it for its own sake, without relating it to function, is utter madness.
ANTHONY BURGESS

Thou hast most traitorously corrupted the youth of the realm in erecting a grammar school. . . . It will be proved to thy face that thou hast men about thee that usually talk of a noun and a verb, and such abominable words as no Christian ear can endure to hear.
WILLIAM SHAKESPEARE, *2 HENRY VI*, 4.7

W hat follows is no tightly systematic theory of grammar. It is merely reliable advice about how to understand the terms in the text, *for the purposes of this text,* and how to identify examples of what they refer to. Each definition has its exceptions, but each remains serviceable for the study of style.

Action: For our purposes, a very broad concept. It includes all movement, feeling, cogitation, creation, attention, etc. Typically, an action is expressed by a verb: *move, hate, think, discover, watch.* Associated with actions are conditions, typically expressed by adjectives: *able, intelligent, plausible, resistant,* etc. But these conditions may also be expressed by nominalizations: *ability, intelligence, plausibility, resistance.*

Active: An active verb usually has the doer of its action as its subject and never occurs in its past participle form after a form of *be.* It may occur in its present participle form after *be.*

I am *checking* the results.

It may occur in its past participle form after *have:*

I have *checked* the results.

A passive verb always has as its subject that which its action is directed toward. It always occurs in its past participle form after a form of *be* (or *get*):

The results have *been checked.*

The results are *being checked.*

Adjective: An adjective qualifies or limits a noun. A word is an adjective if you can put *very* in front of it: *very old, very intelligent, very interesting, very fascinated.* There are exceptions: *major, additional, resumptive, occupational,* etc. You can identify such words as adjectives by trying them out between *the* and an appropriate noun: *The* **occupational** *hazard, the* **major** *reason, an* **additional** *problem,* etc. Unfortunately, because some nouns occur in the same position—*the* **chemical** *hazard*—this method is not always reliable.

Adjective Phrase: An adjective and whatever attaches to it: *so* **large** *that no one could carry it.*

Adverb: This term refers to a potpourri of items. Adverbs modify parts of speech other than nouns. They modify

> Adjectives: **extremely** *large,* **rather** *old,* **very** *tired.*
>
> Verbs: **frequently** *spoke,* **often** *slept,* *left* **here.**
>
> Adverbs: **very** *carefully,* **somewhat** *often,* a bit *late.*
>
> Articles: **precisely** *the man I meant,* **just** *the thing we need.*
>
> Whole sentences: **Fortunately,** *we were on time;*
> **consequently,** we saw the show.

Adverb Phrase: The adverb and whatever attaches to it: *too* **carefully** *to be accidental.*

Agent: The originating force of an action, the source of an action, the responsible party, that entity without which an action could not occur.

Article: *a, an, the, this, that, these, those.*

Clause: Except for imperatives *(Come here!)* a clause has a subject and a verb that can be in a past or present form (it's called a finite verb: *goes, went;* as opposed to an infinitive verb: *to go).* These are all clauses:

> He left.   Why he left
> Because he left   That he left

By this definition, *for him to leave* is not a clause, because the verb *leave* is in its infinitive form, not in its finite form; nor is *his examining the document* a clause, because *examining* cannot be turned into *examined.*

There are two kinds of clauses: *subordinate* and *main* (or *independent*). Subordinate clauses usually begin with subordinating conjunctions.

Adverbial subordinate clauses comment on time, cause, condition, etc. They usually begin with conjunctions such as *because, although, when, if, since, before, as, after, while, unless:*

> **Unless** *you leave,* I will take action.
>
> **Because** *you have not left,* I've called the police.

When *you leave,* close the door.

Adjectival subordinate clauses describe nouns. They are also called relative clauses and usually begin with the relative pronouns *which, that, whom, whose, who:*

The book **that** *I bought for you* was expensive.

My car, **which** *you just saw,* is gone.

A woman **whose** *aunt lives down the street* just called.

We can identify two kinds of relative clauses: restrictive (also called "defining,") and nonrestrictive. A nonrestrictive clause is a clause that is not necessary to identify the noun phrase it modifies. We ordinarily set such a phrase off with commas as a kind of parenthetical addition. A restrictive clause, on the other hand, uniquely identifies the noun it modifies, and ordinarily we do not set such a phrase off with commas because the clause is not parenthetical but necessary. For example, since a person has only one birthday, no modifying phrase can make the phrase *my birthday* any more specific than it already is. So we would set off anything we say about a birthday with commas:

My birthday, **which I keep a secret,** was last month.

This would make no sense:

My birthday **which I keep a secret** was last month.

Such a sentence would suggest that we had more than one birthday, one that we keep secret and at least one other that we don't. On the other hand, a restrictive clause identifies one from among many. For example, if we wanted to distinguish among friends, we would ordinarily require a restrictive clause:

My friends **who live in Ohio** write me every month.

Once we have identified them, however, we use a nonrestrictive clause, since our reader would know to whom we were referring.

These friends, **who in fact know you,** will visit soon.

For a discussion of whether to use *that* or *which,* see p. 193.

Subordinate clauses that function like nouns usually begin with subordinating conjunctions such as *that, what, why, how, who, when, where, whether:*

I don't know **what** *I should do.*

That *she is not here* worries me.

I'll ask **whether** *we can stay.*

I already told you **who** *came.*

In some cases, we can drop the subordinating conjunctions. In this next sentence, the three subordinate clauses are introduced by an adverbial *if,* a relative *which,* and a subordinating conjunction, *that:*

If *we had the resources* **which** *you have described,* I don't doubt **that** *we could do better.*

But we can omit them.

[ ] *Had we the resources* [ ] *you have described,* I don't doubt [ ] *we could do better.*

Main, or independent, clauses have their own subjects and finite verbs and do not function as adjectives, adverbs, or nouns.

Complement: A complement completes a verb that needs completing, that is unfinished without something following it (including direct objects):

	Verb	Complement
I	am	*in the house.*
We	seem	*tired.*
She	discovered	*the money.*
He	began	*to do the job.*

Compound Noun: You can't tell from spelling alone when a pair of words constitutes a compound noun. Some are separate words: *space capsule, retirement home, police station;* some are hyphenated: *mother-*

in-law, eighty-two; some are written as one word: *beehive, airport, book-keeper.* A reliable test is pronunciation: If the first word is stressed more than the second, the word is a compound word: *do͝g ho͝use, spa͝ce c͝apsule, bo͝ok de͝aler.* On the other hand, some phrases that seem to be compounds are stressed on the second word: *g͝arden pa͝th, st͝one wa͝ll, f͝ather co͝nfessor.*

Conjunction: Usually defined as a word that links two other words, phrases, or clauses. But verbs and prepositions do the same thing. It's easier to illustrate conjunctions:

> Adverbial conjunctions: *because, although, when, since, if, unless, while, after,* etc.

> (See *adverbial clause* under Clause.)

> Relative conjunction or relative pronoun: *who, whom, whose, which, that.*

> (See *relative clause* under Clause.)

> Sentence conjunction: *thus, however, therefore, consequently, nevertheless, on the other hand, in fact,* etc.

> Coordinating conjunction: *and, but, yet, for, so, or, nor*

> (See Coordination.)

> Correlative coordinating conjunctions: *both X and Y, not only X but also Y, either X or Y, neither X nor Y, X as well as Y*

Coordination: We coordinate grammatically equal elements:

> Words of the same part of speech: *you* **and** *me, red* **and** *black, run* **or** *jump, old* **yet** *strong*

> Phrases: *In the house* **but** *not in the basement*

> Clauses: *when I leave* **or** *when you arrive*

Ordinarily, the coordinated phrases and clauses have to be of the same grammatical order:

>   Not: *for him to leave* and *that she stayed*
>
>   But: *that he left* and *that she stayed*
>
>   Or: *for him to leave* and *for her to stay*

Correlative Conjunction: See Conjunction. Ordinarily, both members of a pair of correlative conjunctions should introduce a word, phrase, or clause with the same form:

>   Not: He **both** *had the data* **and** *the equipment* to display it.
>
>   But: He had **both** *the data* **and** *the equipment* to display it.
>
>   Not: We will **either** *arrive on Monday* **or** *on Wednesday*.
>
>   But: We will arrive **either** *on Monday* **or** *on Wednesday*.
>
>   Or: We will arrive on **either** *Monday* **or** *Wednesday*.

Direct Object: See Object.

Finite Verb: See Verb.

Free Modifier: A phrase added to the end of a clause that modifies the subject of the clause:

>   She walked along, *ready for anything*. (i.e., she was ready . . .)
>
>   I tried to explain the problem, *pointing out all the difficulties*. (i.e., I pointed out . . .)
>
>   The fire engine appeared, *siren screaming*. (i.e., The fire engine had a siren . . .)

We call it "free" because usually it can also go before the subject:

>   *Ready for anything,* she walked down the street.

Goal: That toward which an action seems to be directed. It may be that which is affected, created, observed, perceived, changed, etc. In most cases, goals are expressed as direct objects. In some cases, the goal can be the subject of an active verb:

I see *you*   *I* underwent an interrogation.

I broke *the dish*   *She* received a warm welcome.

I built *a house*

Grammatical Sentence: A sentence that cannot be separated by a period into two sentences that can stand by themselves without further change. Traditional grammarians call a sentence with a single main clause either *simple* or, if it also contains a dependent clause, *complex:*

Simple: *The bureau* in London *is* no longer responsible for overseas planning, making it a less influential office.

Complex: *The bureau* in London *is* no longer responsible for overseas planning, [because *we have* centralized operations].

Neither of these can be broken into two sentences with a period.

When a punctuated sentence contains more than one grammatical sentence, grammarians call it a *compound sentence* if each of the grammatical sentences consists of a single main clause:

Cleveland won, and Washington lost.

If the punctuated sentence contains two main clauses and one or more subordinate clauses, it is a *compound-complex* sentence:

We stayed because we had paid in advance, but they left.

We can change the first example into two simple sentences and the second into a complex and a simple sentence merely by separating them with periods before *and* and *but.*

Cleveland won. And Washington lost.

We stayed because we had paid in advance. But they left.

The difference between traditional terminology and the terminology

I use here is important: When we talk about "long" sentences, we have to distinguish a long punctuated sentence from a long grammatical sentence. When a long punctuated sentence consists of several grammatical sentences (compound or compound-complex), a reader can usually follow it more easily than she can a long punctuated sentence made up of a single grammatical sentence.

Independent Clause: See Clause.

Infinitive: See Verb.

Intransitive Verb: A verb that does not take an object and cannot be made into a passive verb. These are not transitive verbs:

> He *exists*. They *left* town. She *became* a queen.

Linking Verb: A verb whose complement modifies or refers to the same thing as its subject.

> Linking: He *is* my brother. She *seems* reliable. They *became* teachers. It *appears* broken.

Main Clause: See Clause.

Metadiscourse: Writing about writing. Whatever does not refer to the subject matter being addressed. This includes all connecting devices such as *therefore, however, for example, in the first place;* and all expressions of the author's attitude and intention: *I believe, in my opinion, let me also point out;* all comment about what the writer is about to assert: *most people believe, it is widely assumed, allegedly;* remarks addressed directly to the audience: *as you can see, you will find that, consider now the problem of.*

Nominalization: A noun based on, derived from, communicating the same information as a verb or adjective: *move-movement, act-action, resist-resistance, good-goodness, intelligent-intelligence, elastic-elasticity.*

Nonrestrictive Clause: See Clause.

Noun: A word that will fit into the following: The _____ is good.

Object: There are three kinds of objects: (1) prepositional object: (*in* the house, *by* the walk, *across* the street, *with* fervor); (2) direct object, the noun that follows a transitive verb (I *read* the book, we *followed* the car); (3) indirect object, a noun or pronoun directly after a verb, preceding a direct object: *I gave* him a dollar.

Orienter: A word or phrase, usually at the beginning of a clause, that (1) sets what follows in a time or place, (2) gives the reader a point of view toward what follows, or (3) provides other context that allows a reader to understand an assertion correctly:

> *In the morning,* insects are relatively inactive.

> *Politically speaking,* the Old Left has little influence anymore.

> *Under most circumstances,* mammals protect their young.

Passive: See Active.

Past Participle: Most verbs signal past participle forms with -*ed: jumped, worked, investigated.* Irregular verbs have irregular past participle forms: *seen, broken, swum, stolen, been,* etc. When they follow a *have,* they are in their "perfect" form:

> I *have* **gone.** Her friends *have* **arrived.** We *had* **been** there.

Past participle forms also function as modifiers:

> a *broken* arm, a *twisted* leg, a *scratched* face.

Phrase: A group of words that constitutes a unit but does not contain a subject and a finite verb. There are **noun phrases** that center on a noun and may include modifying elements: *the little* **book** *on the table;* **verb phrases:** *may have been* **found;** and **adjective and adverb phrases.**

Predicate: Roughly, whatever follows the subject. *He* **went downtown yesterday to buy a suit.** Whatever introduces a sentence that could appear with the predicate is also part of the predicate: **Yesterday,** *he* **went downtown.**

Preposition: Roughly, Like conjunctions, prepositions are easier to list than to define: *in, on, up, over, out, under, between, at, toward, with, by, across,* etc.

Prepositional Phrase: The preposition plus its noun object: *in the house, by the door, without enthusiasm.*

Present Participle: The *-ing* form of the verb. It can be used as the *progressive* form of the verb (always following a form of *be*):

> He was *running.* I am *listening.* You *are going.*

Or as a modifier:

> *Running* streams are beautiful. *Working* wives are common.

Or as the *gerund* form, the form that functions as a noun:

> *Running* is good for you. *Listening* is important.

Progressive: See Verb.

Punctuated Sentence: Whatever begins with a capital letter and ends with a period, question mark, or exclamation point.

Relative Clause: See Clause.

Relative Pronoun: See Clause.

Restrictive Clause: See Clause.

Resumptive Modifier: A resumptive modifier is added to the end of a phrase or clause. It repeats a word used at or near the end of that phrase or clause.

> East Coast columnists and commentators delight in expressing their own narrow **view** of the world,
> $$a\ view \ldots$$

To this repeated word more information is added:

> . . . own narrow *view* of the world, *a view shaped by the insular and heated intellectualism that characterizes the East Coast liberal establishment.*

Sentence: There is no easy way to define a *sentence* that would be useful here. It's useful to distinguish two kinds, however: grammatical sentence and punctuated sentence.

Stress: The end of a sentence, where you locate the ideas that you want to emphasize or that you will expand on.

Subject: The subject is whatever the verb agrees with in person and number:

> *Two men are* at the door.

> *One man is* at the door.

We can see that *there* in

> There *was a man* at the door.

> There *were two men* at the door.

is the subject of neither sentence. It is merely a function word that fills the slot that we expect before a verb.

You can always identify a subject once you have identified the verb: Simply put a *who* or a *what* in front of the verb and turn the sentence into a question. The answer to the question is the subject of the sentence:

> That ontogeny recapitulates phylogeny *is* an accepted fact.

> Question: *What* is an accepted fact?

> Answer (and subject): That ontogeny recapitulates phylogeny.

(This doesn't work with sentences beginning with *there*.)

Subordinate Clause: See Clause.

Subordinating Conjunction: *Because, if, when, since, although,* etc.

Summative Modifier: A summative modifier occurs at the end of a clause. It begins by summing up the clause:

> Some believe the price of gold will go to $1,000 an ounce,
> *an opinion . . .*

It then continues with a modifying phrase or clause:

> . . . to $1,000 an ounce,
>   **an opinion** *that is not shared by the rest of us.*

Topic: The idea that a sentence comments on. It is what the sentence is about. The topic is usually the subject of a sentence:

> **China** will eventually become a major industrial nation.

But the topic can appear in other constructions:

> *In regard to* **China**, it will eventually become. . . .

> *I believe that* **China** will eventually become. . . .

> *There is general agreement as to* **China's** eventually becoming a major industrial nation.

Transitive Verb: A verb with a direct object. The object can be made the subject of a passive verb:

> We   ***read***   the book.

> The book   ***was read***   by us.

By this definition, the verbs *resemble, become, stand* (as in *He stands ten feet tall*) are not transitive verbs.

Verb: Verbs have four forms:

Infinitive: The base form of the verb: *go, be, have.* In many cases, the infinitive form follows *to:* He wants *to leave.*

Finite: The verb inflected for present or past: *went, was, were, has, does, sees.* There is no difference between the infinitive and finite forms when the finite form refers to the present and does not have a third-person-*s:*

> I *see* the book.

> I want to *see* the book.

You can always identify the main verb in a clause because it is also the finite form of the verb. To find out which word that is, just change the time the clause refers to. If the clause refers to the past, change it to refer to the present; if to the present, change it to the past; if to the future, to either past or present. The word you have to change is the finite verb:

He *decided* to leave.	He *decides* to leave.
He *left*.	He *leaves*.

The two other forms are the perfect and the progressive. Most English verbs use the -*ed* form for the perfect:

> He has walk*ed;* I have danc*ed;* you have stumbl*ed*.

But many verbs have irregular forms:

> She has s*u*ng; they were beat*en;* we have g*one*.

The progressive form always ends in -*ing:*

> They were danc*ing,* walk*ing,* and sing*ing*.

Some Possible Revisions to the Exercises

Few of the exercises in this book have a single correct answer. A good many of your answers will be different from but as good as those here; indeed, I would be surprised if many were not better. Trust your ear. If you decide your version is better than the answer here, try to state why: Don't depend on generalities like clarity and precision. Try to say *why* it's clearer and more precise: Is it shorter? Is it more specific? If your answers are less compact and direct than those suggested here, try to decide whether the difference between your version and mine is a significant difference. There comes a point in every sentence where another five minutes spent looking for the most concise and specific version possible is simply not worth the result. It's the first thirty seconds that count.

Exercise 2–1

1. We expected to establish new tolerance levels.
3. The governing committee announced that they would submit their report by the deadline.
5. The governor must refuse the request.
7. At that time, independent investigators measured the half-life of thorium more accurately.
9. The business sector did not independently analyze what caused the trade deficit. (did not attempt to analyze why trade was in the red)
11. Management was uneasy over the result of the survey.
13. The insurer must check the discrepancy in the data.
15. The police immediately investigated the affair.
17. After the last report, we studied the same principles of bilateral symmetry.

19. I believe that the administrators should consult with the student body before anyone changes the rules.

21. They must redetermine what personnel they need before local sources can assist them.

23. When the President recently asserted that the press was chronically unable to present information accurately and fairly, he insightfully described the way the press reports events in the Middle East. If we compare how the press covers different events in the region, we can recognize how those events are inaccurately reported by American journalists, particularly those associated with certain politically biased newspapers. They omit facts, they exaggerate local conflicts, they slant facts. These actions all show how the press has failed to carry out its mission in the independent way we expect of American newspaper reporters. As a consequence, because Americans lack accurate knowledge of the events of the area, they form opinions on the basis of their emotions, not their reason.

Exercise 2-2

1. I have reanalyzed your figures in order to determine the coefficient of error. I will announce the results when I judge the situation to be appropriate. (How would this differ if the subjects were some third person? i.e., "Smith has reanalyzed your figures . . . he will announce . . . when he judges . . .")

3. Trotsky abandons his usual impassioned narrative style and puts in its place a cautious and scholarly treatment of theories of conspiracy (and instead, treats theories of conspiracy in a cautious and scholarly way). But the moment he picks up his narrative line again, he invests his prose. . . .

5. Almost certainly, we would want to know who has been ignoring the wiretapping regulation: For many years federal, state, and local law enforcement agencies (individuals?) have been regularly ignoring wiretapping restrictions. We know that only the Court or Congress can impose restrictions, so the agent of *impose* is probably irrelevant.

7. We have written these technical directives as simply as possible because we are attempting to communicate more effectively with relatively uneducated employees whom we have hired in accordance with guidelines imposed on us by the federal government.

9. The researchers evaluated tissue rejection according to procedures that most other researchers have abandoned because those procedures consistently overestimated values for the production of antibodies (because those procedures consistently led them to overestimate values for . . .).

11. We may most accurately frame the problem of how to reform the schools if we attempt to analyze completely and fairly how schooling/education/teachers cultivate reasoning/help a child learn to reason.

13. We have omitted from this dictionary a handful of old, well-known vulgate terms for sexual and excretory organs and functions not because current literature does not contain them/because we could not find citations for them in current literature. On the contrary, in recent years, because people have used these terms so often that everyone now knows what they mean, we don't have to explain them. As we culled words—the inevitable task of any lexicographer—we decided to eliminate them on practical grounds: people in many quarters object to seeing these terms in print. If we introduced these terms, people in those quarters might try to keep this dictionary out of the hands of some students. We would have been unwise to risk that possibility.

Exercise 2-3

1. The committee on standards for plant safety discussed recent announcements of regulations regarding air quality.

3. Phenomena involving the pancreatic gland are regulated chiefly by cells in the parasympathetic nervous system.

5. On the basis of these principles, we may now attempt to formulate rules by which we extract information from narratives.

7. The Federal Trade Commission is responsible for enforcing federal guidelines about the durability of tires on new cars.

9. The Social Security program guarantees a standard floor for monthly income for individuals whose package of potential benefits is determined by what those individuals have contributed over the course of their lives.

11. Because state law supervises the organization of corporations (how corporations are organized), the federal government is unable to effectively implement measures that would reduce pollution.

13. On November 1, 1979, the secretary of the Department of Energy announced in a press release that after the Department of Energy and major manufacturers met on October 28 to discuss the matter, the manufacturers decided to dispose of their surplus stock of alcohol.

15. In order to interpret cardiac sounds, one must know intimately cardiac physiology and the pathophysiology of cardiac disease.

Exercise 3-1

1. In his classic paper on children's thinking, Jones (1985) stressed that how well a child solved problems depended crucially on how well the child used language. According to Jones, when children improve their language skills, they also improve their ability to solve non-verbal problems. He suggested that children performed better because they were able to use their previously acquired language habits to articulate the problem and then to activate knowledge that they had previously learned through language. Therefore, if we have children practice formulating non-linguistic problems in speech before they attempt to solve the problems, we might enhance their ability to solve problems in general/they might learn to solve problems better in general.

3. Except in those areas continually covered with ice or scorched by continual heat, the earth is covered with vegetation. Plants grow not only in richly fertilized plains and river valleys but at the edge of perpetual snow in high mountains, not only in and around lakes and swamps but under the ocean and next to it. They survive in the cracks of busy city sidewalks as well as in barren rocks. Vegetation covered the earth before we existed and will cover the earth after evolution swallows us up.

5. [I have tried to change the nominalization *behavior* into the verb *behave* simply as an exercise. We could easily change all the clauses with *behave* as a verb back into the nominalization *behavior* because that concept is the topic of this passage, a concept that the writer refers to often enough to require its own noun. If you have used *behave* as a verb more than two or three times, try changing it back to the nominalization.] Educators reflect theories about behavior in two ways. First, school officials issue edicts that require teachers to stipulate what they want their children to learn in terms of how they

want the children to behave or (that is?), in terms of what those teachers can observe in the behavior of the children that the teachers will count as showing the children have learned what the teachers want them to learn. Second, the literature suggests that teachers use behavioral theory as method to teach the children/get the children to learn/modify the way children behave, a use that stresses reinforcement schedules/schedules that reinforce behavior. Apparently, these educators/theorists assume that they can explain the way humans act in terms of what causes them to act, that they can observe the way humans think and feel if they observe the way humans publicly behave, and that if they manipulate what causes people to behave in certain ways, they can alter the way they behave.

Exercise 3-2

1. Your car may have a defective part. This part connects the suspension to the frame. If it fails, you won't be able to steer, especially if you brake hard. We may also have to adjust the secondary latch on your hood because we may have misaligned it. If you don't latch the primary latch, the secondary latch might not hold the hood down. If the hood flies up while you are driving, you won't be able to see. If either of these things occurs, you could crash and no one will warn you.

Exercise 3-3

There are many possible answers to this problem. Here are only a few.

1. The people of this village hear something from the cathedral at Chartres which I do not; but it is important to understand that I hear something from this cathedral which they cannot. Perhaps they respond in awe to (this makes the villagers the agents of the action) ...; Perhaps the power of the spires, the glory of the windows strike them (this makes the topic the power of the spires, etc., but keeps *power*... as the seeming agent), but God has made Himself known to them longer than to me. .... I recoil in terror from the slippery bottomless well (this makes Baldwin the agent of the action); the slippery bottomless well... terrifies me (this makes the well and the

gargoyles the topic of the sentence but keeps them as the agents of the action). I doubt that the devil ever occurs to the villagers when the cathedral faces them . . . because they have never identified themselves with the devil/because the devil has never been identified with them. . . .

But the status which I derive from myth in the West imposes itself on me before the myth will change.

3.   On June 30, 1986, Owens Accounting hired William Smith. . . . At that time, George Owens explained to Smith that he would promote Smith to . . . if Owens judged that Smith's performance was at the level of competence Owens expected of other Auditors. Owens directly supervised Smith in this position and carefully observed him. Owens believes that Smith's progress was not as rapid as appropriate. Owens did not meet with Smith to inform him about how he had evaluated him. On January 3, 1987, Owens met with Smith and told him that he would not advance Smith to Permanent Auditor . . . until Owens was satisfied with Smith's performance of his job. Owens advised Smith that he was available to help Smith master the job, if desired. According to Smith, Owens unreasonably surprised him when Owens informed him that he had been accumulating negative observations about him that would lead Owens to delay his promotion. Owens gave Smith no reason to believe that Owens was not satisfied with Smith's performance, and Owens had given him no occasion to learn that fact. Smith now. . . .

Exercise 4-1

1.   The most significant danger to the republic is the judiciary's tendency to rewrite the Constitution.

3.   In large American colleges and universities, opportunities for teachers to work with individual students are limited/teachers have limited opportunities to work with individual students.

5.   Along with the aforementioned summary, we present several studies that evaluate upper and lower eyelid reconstruction.

7.   College students commonly complain about teachers who assign a long term paper and then give only a grade.

9.   In required courses that do not change textbooks every year, it would be economically feasible for students to rent books rather than buy them.

11. A different question is how to dispose of materials that do not biodegrade.

13. DuPage County, sixteen miles west of the Loop and covering 338 square miles, has the fastest growing population in the region.

Exercise 4-2

1. During the reign of Queen Elizabeth, a popular story was that of King Lear and his three daughters (or for an audience who is entirely familiar with *King Lear:* the story of King Lear and his three daughters was a popular story). By the time Elizabeth died, it was available in a dozen easily accessible books. But most of these stories were simple narratives that stated rather obvious morals and that failed to develop the characters. Several versions of this story must have been known to Shakespeare when he began work on *Lear,* one of his greatest tragedies. But while he based his characters on the stock figures of the legend, he turned them into credible human beings with complex motives.

3. The most important event in Thucydides' *History of the Peloponnesian War* is Athens' catastrophic Sicilian Invasion. He devotes three-quarters of his history to setting it up/Thucydides sets it up through the first three-quarters of his history. In particular, we can see how Thucydides anticipated the Invasion by the way he describes the step-by-step decline in Athenian Society. Why did he do this? He did this because he wanted to make it seem as inevitable as the climax in a Greek tragic drama. (Now that the information is in the right order, we can combine these sentences: Because the most important event, . . . he devotes three-quarters . . . In particular we can see how Thucydides anticipated the Invasion by describing a step-by-step decline in Athenian society to make the Invasion seem as inevitable as the climax in a Greek tragic drama.)

5. Revenue has changed as follows for the period July 1–August 31. The Ohio and Kentucky areas increased their net from $32,934 to $56,792, approximately 73%. Indiana and Illinois increased their net from $153,281 to $168,651, or 10%. However, revenues from Wisconsin and Minnesota decreased from $200,102 to $190,580, or approximately 5%. (On the other hand, if the actual numbers were more important, then the actual numbers might come last.)

Exercise 5-1

1. The agencies that assist participants in our programs have reversed their recently announced policy to return to their original one.
3. Science depends on accurate data if it is to offer ideas that will allow mankind to advance safely.
5. Most patients at public clinics probably accept general medical treatment because their problems are rather minor and can be treated with understanding and attention.

Exercise 5-2

1. Graduate students looking for good teaching jobs face an uncertain future.
3. When investors believe that inflation will continue to grow, they usually invest in works of art.
5. The most important problem is how much the characters disguise the social tensions in the playwright's society.

Exercise 5-3

1. But TV programming will probably continue to appeal to our most prurient interests.
3. The person we call Shakespeare could be someone else, perhaps even royalty.
5. Finally, China is a good example of a country that is on the verge of a major industrial expansion.
7. I do not believe that unexplored parts of the world have snakes larger than those we already know about.
9. The family and other institutions are perhaps even more important than education as transmitters of social values.

Exercise 5-4

1. Inflation will continue if the federal government keeps on spending.
3. Scientists disagree whether the universe is open or closed, a dispute

they will resolve only when they have computed the total mass of the universe with an error of no more than 5 percent.

5. We must develop tar sand, oil shale, and coal as sources of fuel, because we must make ourselves invulnerable to foreign powers that at any moment might cut off our oil.

7. We can treat cancer effectively only if we remove the tumor before it metastasizes.

9. When elections deal with those issues that normally escape attention, they will serve their intended function.

11. Stop taking the medicine only if you are still dizzy and nauseated six hours after you started taking it.

13. You will be prohibited from participating in the cost-sharing education programs only after you have had a hearing into why you were rejected.

Exercise 5-5

1. When we look at advertising systematically, we logically begin by defining the term. This establishes a shared point of reference that lets us approach the topic objectively. Unfortunately, because we must define advertising in so many ways, it makes it likely that we will be subjective. That indicates that we must examine popular notions about advertising carefully.

Exercise 6-1

1. Responding to the problems we identified in our self-study, this college has already created many activities that meet the expanding needs and interests of our students. These new programs also reflect the traditional goals of the college: the liberal education of the whole person.

3. It is true that because responsibility is unclearly defined in this organization, its training program has a long history of financial problems and disputes among management. But it is equally true that in the last few years it has placed approximately half of its trainees in jobs equal to their abilities.

5.   Many people have decided to give up on life in the city because they are defeated by its dirt and its crime, even though when they leave they realize that they will miss its intensity and excitement.

7.   In this procedure, we assume that our sample is large enough to include the variation that we would find in the larger population, that in our statistical analysis, we follow accepted procedures, and that we can replicate the study under conditions like those in similar studies.

9.   For a corporation to obligate itself to another party upon a contract, the other party must prove the following: (1) The corporation or its authorized agent acted to accept the contract, or (2) the Board of Directors adopted and ratified the contract. A court will assume that the corporation ratified the contract if it acquiesced in or accepted any of the benefits of the contract. It is essential to such implied ratification that when the corporation accepted the contract, it knew all the pertinent facts.

Exercise 7–1

The answers are only exemplary, of course.

1.   Many school systems are returning to the basics, basics that have been too long ignored . . . a change that will be welcomed by parents everywhere . . . reasserting the old values that have been ignored for too long.

3.   Why we age is a matter that has puzzled humanity for millennia, a matter that is just now being unraveled . . . a mystery that is just now being unraveled . . . inspiring questions that go to the heart of the human condition.

5.   The recent fertilization of an embryo in a test tube has raised ethical issues that are troubling both scientists and laypeople, issues that go to the very center of how we define life and humanity . . . an event that will influence both religious and scientific thinking.

7.   In 1961, the U.S. government announced that it would put the first man on the moon, a decision that proved to be one of the best we ever made.

9.   In the 1960s, the Supreme Court ruled that anyone arrested for a crime had to be given the widest benefit of legal doubt, a view not

shared by the law enforcement officers who had to deal with crime more directly.

11. Systematic skepticism denies that we can ever know reality so long as it is screened by human perception, perception that changes reality before we can even begin to contemplate it or even to think about it ... a point of view that denies both the accuracy of our senses and the intelligence of our minds.

13. During the Renaissance, affluent and politically stable scientists allowed streams of thought to flow together, streams of thought that had both political consequences for every government and intellectual consequences for every European culture ... a development that changed not only the future but the past as well.

Exercise 7–2

1. Because Congress failed to anticipate the cost of inflation when it originally voted funds for the Interstate Highway System, the system has run into insoluble problems, problems that could spell the end of the most extensive construction project in world history.

3. Because TV game shows appeal to the cupidity in us all, they are just about the most popular daytime TV, a fact that does not bode well for evening TV.

5. Working with devices that can accelerate particles almost to the speed of light, researchers in high-energy physics are exploring the ultimate nature of matter, providing us with ever more puzzling facts about the basis of physical existence.

7. If before the next congressional election the government does not provide all political candidates with campaign funds, only the rich will be able to seek public office in numbers large enough to assure a wide selection of candidates, numbers that will not, however, include a wide range of political views.

9. In the last half century medical science has learned to detect and even to anticipate diseases that would formerly have appeared in our midst and devastated whole populations; it can now predict the outbreak of diseases such as influenza a year in advance, allowing us to prepare for their onslaught.

Exercise 7-3

1. They submitted an ecological impact statement identical to that of the previous year, so it will again be difficult for us to evaluate their data, because we still have no information independently verifying what they supplied.

3. Because we have reorganized the division for marketing research, information more accurate than that which we have received in the past should allow us to identify populations different from those we have traditionally aimed at. This information will be relatively easy to analyze because we have already accumulated demographic data such as average income, spending patterns, etc., for many different markets. As a result, we may expect an operation more efficient than that which we conducted last year.

Exercise 7-4

1. However, according to many other reports, children in early grades have higher achievement scores because, as a nation, we have improved the way we prepare disadvantaged children before they begin school.

3. With little sense of scholarly bias, historians impose on the past not just their private view of historical relevancy but the implied view of their whole social matrix.

5. The next point is the isolation of various clotting mechanisms in higher mammals.

7. It is universally acknowledged that when Woodrow Wilson refused to take into his confidence the leadership of the United States Senate, he caused the defeat of the Treaty of Versailles.

9. Last year in England, though, there was discovered a virus that bears no known relation to any other form of protein-based life.

11. Because we were unfamiliar with the mechanism, we were not able to detect any metal with it.

13. Because the students realized that the undergraduate curriculum had to be revised in the next few weeks, they put proposals on the agenda that had been discussed earlier.

Exercise 8–1

1. Those who keep silent over the loss of small freedoms will eventually find themselves being kept silent by the loss of large ones.
3. We should pay more attention to those politicians who tell us how to risk making what we have better than to those who tell us how to keep whatever we have from getting worse.
5. Too many teachers mistake neat papers rehashing conventional ideas for careful logic supporting unexpected truths.
7. Never mistake a style that is too difficult to penetrate for ideas that are too complex to understand.
9. This report does not adequately balance the importance of our immediate cash flow against the need to increase the size of our funded reserves.

Exercise 8–2

1. Few tendencies in our government have changed American life more than the unrestricted power of federal agencies.
3. The day is past when boards of education can expect taxpayers to automatically go along with the decisions of extravagant administrators.
5. If we invest our sweat in these projects, we must not seem to be working out of self-interest.
7. Throughout history, science has advanced because dedicated scientists have overcome the hostility of an uninformed public.

Exercise 8–3

1. The figures in the first quarter report point to some important facts about productivity, especially how hidden costs are forcing us to cut back our research budget. They reveal how much we need even more research into ways to stop the spiralling wages of unskilled labor.
3. We should not too devoutly hope that because we are rational we can make empty space part of our vision of the universe and of our place in it. We will fail because our animal nature prevents us from fully accepting the fact that we are mortal in a transient existence.

Exercise 9-1

1. From all available evidence no black man had ever set foot in this tiny Swiss village before I came. I was told before arriving that I would probably be a "sight" for the village; I took this to mean that people of my complexion were rarely seen in Switzerland, and also that city people are always something of a "sight" outside of the city. It did not occur to me—possibly because I am an American—that there could be people anywhere who had never seen a Negro.

    It is a fact that cannot be explained on the basis of the inaccessibility of the village. The village is very high, but it is only four hours from Milan and three hours from Lausanne. It is true that it is virtually unknown. Few people making plans for a holiday would elect to come here. On the other hand, the villagers are able, presumably, to come and go as they please—which they do: to another town at the foot of the mountain, with population of approximately five thousand, the nearest place to see a movie or go to the bank. In the village there is no movie house, no bank, no library, no theater; very few radios, one jeep, one station wagon; and at the moment, one typewriter, mine, an invention which the woman next door to me here had never seen. There are about six hundred people living here, all Catholic—I conclude this from the fact that the Catholic church is open all year round, whereas the Protestant chapel, set off on a hill a little removed from the village, is open only in the summertime when the tourists arrive. There are four or five hotels, all closed now, and four or five bistros, of which, however, only two do any business during the winter. These two do not do a great deal, for life in the village seems to end around nine or ten o'clock. There are a few stores, butcher, baker, *épicerie,* a hardware store, and a money-changer—who cannot change travelers' checks, but must send them down to the bank, an operation which takes two or three days. There is something called the Ballet Hall, closed in the winter and used for God knows what, certainly not ballet, during the summer. There seems to be only one schoolhouse in the village, and this for the quite young children.

STYLE

Finally, there should grow the most austere of all mental qualities; I mean the sense for style. It is an aesthetic sense, based on admiration for the direct attainment of a foreseen end, simply and without waste. Style in art, style in literature, style in science, style in logic, style in practical execution have fundamentally the same aesthetic qualities, namely, attainment and restraint. The love of a subject in itself and for itself, where it is not the sleepy pleasure of pacing a mental quarter-deck, is the love of style as manifested in that study. Here we are brought back to the position from which we started, the utility of education. Style, in its finest sense, is the last acquirement of the educated mind; it is also the most useful. It pervades the whole being. The administrator with a sense for style hates waste; the engineer with a sense for style economizes his material; the artisan with a sense for style prefers good work. Style is the ultimate morality of mind.

ALFRED NORTH WHITEHEAD
THE AIMS OF EDUCATION

Acknowledgments

Excerpt from *Notes of a Native Son* by James Baldwin. Copyright © 1955 by James Baldwin. Reprinted by permission of Beacon Press and Michael Joseph Ltd.

D. H. Lawrence, *Studies in Classic American Literature.* New York: The Viking Press, 1961

Norman Mailer, *Armies of the Night.* New York: The New American Library, Inc., 1971.

From *Science and the Common Understanding* by J. Robert Oppenheimer. Copyright © 1954 by J. Robert Oppenheimer, renewed © 1981 by Robert B. Meyner. Reprinted by permission of Simon & Schuster, Inc.

Excerpt from Foreword, *Webster's New World Dictionary,* Second College Edition, 1974, p. viii. Copyright © 1974 by William Collins + World Publishing Company. Reprinted by permission of Simon & Schuster, Inc.

From "The Aims of Education" in *The Aims of Education and Other Essays* by Alfred North Whitehead. Copyright © 1929 by Macmillan Publishing Co., Inc., renewed 1957 by Evelyn Whitehead. Reprinted by permission.

INDEX